the FRENCH experience

Tutor's Guide

Duncan Sidwell

Bernard Kavanagh

BBC BOOKS

The French Experience 1 course book, audio cassettes or CDs, Activity Book
Tutor's Guide and Tutor's Cassette pack are linked to the content of the BBC TV
and Radio language series *The French Experience 1.*

TV and radio programmes first broadcast autumn 1994.

Television producer: David Wilson
Radio producer: Mick Webb
Audio producer: Alan Wilding, BBC Language Unit

Developed by the BBC Language Unit
Edited by Harriette Lanzer
Proofread by Véronique Bussolin
Designed by Simon Bell for Book Creation Services Ltd, London
Typeset by Gene Ferber for Book Creation Services Ltd, London
Illustrations and artwork by Sylvie Rabbe and Beatrice Reis Custodio
     for Book Creation Services Ltd, London

ISBN 0 563 39900 7

Published by BBC Books, a division of BBC Enterprises Ltd
Woodlands, 80 Wood Lane, London W12 0TT
First published 1994

Printed and bound in Great Britain by Clays Ltd, St Ives Plc

Contents

INTRODUCTION

[A]
The course

The French Experience is a multi-media course for beginners learning French. It is designed to meet the varied needs of adult learners, whether studying independently or in classes. The course aims to take learners to a level roughly equivalent to GCSE or NVQ level 1.

[B]
The components

As well as this Tutor's Guide, the course consists of:
* 288-page, full-colour Student Book: contains 16 main teaching units, four units for revision and assessment and four extension units (17–20) which consolidate and widen the language learned in the previous units. The fully-comprehensive reference section includes an answer key, tapescript, language summary and French-English glossary.

* Four 75-minute Student Audio Cassettes or CDs: closely integrated with the Student Book. Two presenters talk students through the new material in English. A series of activities focus first on listening and recognising, then on speaking. Most of the conversations and interviews were recorded in various locations in France.

* 80-page Activity Book: closely linked to each unit of the Student Book, providing extra practice in reading and writing.

* Two 90-minute Tutor's Cassettes: contain all the French conversations and interviews without the English explanations or the role-plays.

[C]
Tutor's Guide

This guide provides suggestions and materials for use in the classroom, principally to encourage speaking. There are suggestions for homework and two assessment units are provided. Each block within the 20 units is presented separately with:
* objectives
* key language
* grammar
* teaching suggestions
The suggestions for teaching include the use of cue cards, worksheets and overhead transparencies as well as ideas for the use of audio and visual materials.

[D]
General approach of the Tutor's Guide

The main aim of the guide is to provide ideas to encourage communication among students. This involves a gradual build-up of language and the use of simple visual aids, such as symbols or key words. You are encouraged to use French as much as possible in your teaching.

The final aim of each block is to give students the opportunity to talk to each other with the minimum of written support. Cue card activities (see [F] below), if completed successfully, can demonstrate that the speaking objectives of the block have been achieved.

You are encouraged to use pairwork or small groupwork for the exchange of information and opinions and for language games. These are generally led into with visual cues or cue words which provide support with communicating. The audio and visual materials are an essential part of the learners' progression and in each block suggestions are given as to how these may be exploited.

[E]
Encouraging communication in pairs

The teaching notes encourage you to use information gap activities. These activities are important in enabling learners to feel confident in speaking since they require them to pass information to each other. This also means that learners have to ask questions – something that usually needs a great deal of practice. As well as practising students in asking questions, these activities allow speakers to express themselves in their own words.

In doing these activities students may have to pretend to be someone else, to invent details about someone or something or to take part in imagined situations, e.g. being at the bank or in a shop. You clearly need to use fictitious situations in order to practise a full range of language a number of times.

Listeners will frequently be encouraged to note down what their partners say in order to check it back or to enable them to take part in report back sessions as a whole group activity.

[F]
Using cue cards

An example of cue cards and the type of dialogues which may be derived from them is given below.

Students can exchange information in pairs about their name, nationality, job, marital status and partner's name. The student decides the age and job of the partner plus any further details they want. In making and using such cue cards you need to check that the student can ask the necessary questions and that the symbols or words used for the cues are clear.

> **Student A**
> Paul
> angl
> architecte
> mar – Yvonne
>
> Yvonne: prof?

> **Student B**
> Sylvie
> f
> journaliste
> cél – Michel
>
> Michel: prof?

Although both students know the general theme of what they will talk about, neither knows the actual content of the other's card. Each student will need to ask questions to obtain information and will also need to pay attention to what the other is saying. Each may need to seek clarification or ask for repetition and so you need to make sure that you teach the necessary language: *Vous pouvez répéter? Je n'ai pas compris.*

The information on these cards is quite extensive and the manner in which it is presented does not restrict the speaker to any particular level of language. Students can both add details and speak at a more complex level if desired. The dialogue derived from the above cue cards could go something like this:

A: *Vous vous appelez comment?*
B: *Moi, je m'appelle Sylvie. Vous êtes anglais?*
A: *Oui. Et vous?*
B: *Je suis française. Qu'est-ce que vous faites comme métier?*
A: *Je suis architecte.*
B: *Moi, je suis journaliste.*
A: *Vous êtes mariée?*
B: *Non. Célibataire. Je vis avec mon ami, Michel. Il est journaliste aussi. Vous êtes marié?*
A: *Oui. Ma femme est professeur. Elle s'appelle Yvonne.*

Clearly this dialogue could have taken many other forms. The questions could have been put differently and the way the information was given could have been varied. It could have been conducted as two interviews, for example. The essential point is that the participants had the choice of how to do this and the challenge to

make it work. They were not reading a script. Having achieved the task they knew that they were actually capable of carrying out this exchange. Learners could do a number of cards, assuming different personalities in order to practise the language thoroughly.

[G]
Getting feedback

You could have asked the students to note the information from the cue cards above so that everyone then reports back, giving the details of the last person they spoke with.

T: *Et alors, vous voulez bien présenter votre partenaire, Judy? Je note les détails ici au tableau.*
J: *Eu... Il s'appelle Henri. Il est chauffeur de taxi. Il est...*

In this way the language is heard once more (in the third person) and spoken in public so that you can hear, check and assist. You can also take feedback in the first person singular of course, if that is what you want to reinforce at the time.

T: (to Judy) *Et alors...Vous, madame. Vous vous appelez comment? ...*

Note that at this stage there is no prepared dialogue read from a book. Each participant really does have to use his/her own linguistic resources to complete the task and each is dependent on the other. There is no reason why students should not have practised 'set piece' model dialogues at an earlier stage of the learning, but such dialogues do not in themselves constitute communicative practice.

A second point to note is that you and your students need to become used to using cue words and symbols in order to stimulate dialogues at this stage. These techniques will be used in this Tutor's Guide, and you can of course develop your own.

[H]
Using choice frameworks

One technique which is suggested at times in this Tutor's Guide allows you to give communicative practice to the whole group. This is done through choice frameworks (see below). An advantage of this technique is that the students can have a choice in what they say, while at the same time other students are placed in the position of being a genuine listener – they do not know what is going to be said and therefore need to pay attention. By working in this way with the whole group you have the opportunity to check, correct and assist the learners on their way to speaking confidently. The choice framework below covers the same language area as the cue cards in [F].

Nom	Nationalité	Profession	Relation
Yves	f	journaliste	divorcé(e)
Yvonne	it	professeur	marié(e)
Larry	port	chauffeur	séparé(e)
Luisa	angl	– de taxi	veuve/-f
Giuseppe	aust	– de camion	cél
Jane	dan	ingénieur	ami(e)
Klaus	all	secrétaire	
Eva	gr		
Alessandra	rus		
Jutta			

If this choice framework were used as a worksheet or, better, put on the OHP at a point in the learning when the class had some familiarity with most of the words, then a large number of statements could be made. Students could either talk about 'themselves' or create personalities. The choice framework could also be used for:

* Listening – you make statements and the students note the detail and then report it back later: *Giuseppe est italien. Il est ingénieur et il est divorcé. Il vit avec une amie, qui s'appelle Eva et qui est danoise. Eva est secrétaire.*
* Speaking – you and the class make statements about 'themselves' or other people whom they pretend to know: *Alors, je m'appelle Larry. Je suis australien et je suis chauffeur de camion. Je suis marié et ma femme...* or *J'ai un ami/frère/une sœur... Il/Elle s'appelle...*

There could also be an interchange in the class where students are encouraged to ask each other about themselves or their friends.

T: *Je commence. Alors, comment vous appelez-vous?*
S1: *Je m'appelle Alessandra.*
S2: *De quelle nationalité êtes-vous?*
S1: *Je suis italienne.*
S3: *Qu'est-ce que vous faites dans la vie?*

T: *Je vais commencer. Sandra, votre frère, il s'appelle comment?*
S: *Il s'appelle Klaus.*
S2: *Il est anglais?*
S: *Non, il est allemand. Je suis allemande. Je m'appelle Jutta.*
S3: *Et quelle est votre profession?*

In these examples it would be possible for you to help those that need it and provide new words if students wanted to use them. The students are able to use their imagination yet are also given some ideas to work with. The structures which carry the vocabulary are constantly being re-presented to them by the statements that others make. They need to pay attention to this re-presentation of language because its content is unpredictable and they are required to note it, or to respond to it.

Notice that abbreviated forms of the nationalities have been used here as an illustration of what can be done in the way of giving partial support. Symbols could even be used for the jobs once the language was beginning to be known. Once this sort of practice had been done with the whole class, the students could have cue cards and work in pairs, again perhaps noting the information for a later feedback session.

[I]
Using audio tapes

Audio forms an integral part of the course. Clearly it is a major learning resource which can be used in many ways:

* Modelling language – in each block, new material is presented partly by means of the audio tape. It serves as a model for pronunciation, intonation, rhythm, the pattern of a dialogue giving a model to copy and new phrases.

When you use such material some repetition is helpful, provided of course the students understand the meaning.

T: *Vous vous appelez comment?*
F: *Frank Martin.*
T: *Où est-ce que vous travaillez?*
F: *Je travaille au tennis club de Montbrison, dans le département de la Loire, en France.*
T: *Et qu'est-ce que vous faites exactement?*
F: *Je suis professeur de tennis.*

With this you could proceed in the following way:
1. Play the tape.
2. Ask for any information that the students can give you.
3. Establish meanings they are not sure of by playing it through a little at a time.
4. Encourage them to repeat the dialogue little by little.
5. Go over it again asking: *Qu'est-ce qu'il/elle dit?* just before you play a phrase. As students progress, use more complex language: *Demandez son nom. Demandez où il travaille/habite. Demandez une précision.*

When they have got the hang of the dialogue, begin to change it, offering possibilities on the board or asking students to provide them – the name can change, the job can be different, etc. You may then want to look at the text. Alternatively, you may want to look at the text first, close books and then go through the sort of procedure outlined above.

The same techniques can be used with video tapes. If your educational institution is licensed by the Educational Recording Agency you may record the television broadcasts to use in class.

[J]
The use of the text with written script

For many students it is helpful to see the written word at the same time as hearing it. This increases the input of language so that they may absorb more by seeing and hearing. Of course, if your purpose is to practise them in sorting out meaning from what they hear, or to concentrate on the sound only then you would just wish to play the tape. This point is made in order to illustrate the main point of using tape (and video) – that is, the use depends upon a careful analysis of what you as a tutor want the nature of the learning to be.

[K]
Teaching or testing?

A frequent use of audio (or video) is to test comprehension. This is often done in the mistaken belief that it increases learning. It may possibly do so in some circumstances, but in many cases it is really a test from which the student learns little. It is not uncommon that an audio (or video) tape is played, questions are asked or read and then the students note how many questions they got right or wrong. If you want students to absorb and be able to use language from a tape they need to hear it/see it a number of times. This means that you need to go over it with them in a variety of ways so that they 'overlearn' without becoming bored. Each time they hear it they need to have a different activity so that they go deeper into the language and so that they are presented with a number of opportunities to learn. This may not be very extensive at elementary levels, but it is still possible.

[L]
Techniques

When using audio (or video) it is helpful for students to see or hear the whole extract first before you begin to do language work with it. However, you should also bear in mind that it is generally best to select short extracts and obtain student reaction or do an activity of some sort after only a short period of listening/viewing. This will enable you to concentrate on language rather than having your students' attention being drawn to too a wide range of things.

When using either audio or video invite impressions or any information students can give you. This will enable them to talk and will indicate to you what is known and what is not known. Students may therefore talk about the colour of something, an event, whom they saw or heard, the weather, etc. Remember that the tense used will be relevant here – il pleuvait may be beyond them while il pleut may not be, in which case you will need to use the pause or still button carefully. You can ask questions about the general drift of the tape, e.g. where it is, how many people there are, whether the speakers are men or women.

[M]
Using the pause, stop and rewind buttons for linguistic work

Some of these suggestions apply both to video and to audio tape. Having viewed/listened to the extract and then isolated certain expressions for study, you can invite students to:
* predict – pause the tape just before someone speaks and ask what he/she says
* recall immediately – pause the tape and ask what someone has said
* give simultaneous commentary – use the volume control and ask students to give any language that they can recall to fit the action
* transcribe very short parts of the text while you use the pause button.

[N]
Using text and the tape

You can use the tape transcript for study of language:
* take the transcript and use it to clarify parts which may be difficult to get aurally
* alter the transcript and invite students to spot the differences – these can be changes of fact/expressions, or the text can be rearranged
* replace parts of the text you have cut from the transcript.

[O]
Other language work

Ask students to:
* spot certain words
* note certain words from a list which includes some redundant words – let students tell you about the tape rather than questioning them first and when they talk abut it ask if they noticed the word for this or that before replaying the tape to check their answers
* find expressions used in the tape which are similar in meaning to some that you give them on paper
* reconstruct language of parts of the episode viewed or heard – this can be a group activity
* listen to a short extract and then say something similar – they hear: Mon père a 58 ans. Il est né en Espagne. They say: Mon père a 67 ans et il est né en Italie.

[P]
Noughts and crosses

A useful strategy for introducing new vocabulary is for students to play noughts and crosses in groups of three. Two play noughts and crosses in the usual way, identifying where they want their cross or nought to go in Grid B by saying a word or, in the example below, a number from Grid A. The third student writes a nought or cross in the corresponding square in Grid B. For example, if Student 1 says *vingt-quatre*, Student 3 writes a nought in the top left-hand square, and so on.

24	36	42
51	18	64
78	94	81

Grid A

Grid B

Many things can be practised in this way, e.g. *ton, ta, tes*. Grid A has nouns in it – *frère, sœur, parents,* for example, the speaker identifies the square for Student 3 who writes in the nought or cross in Grid B. If the students say *ton parents* or *mon sœur* they miss a go.

BIENVENUE!

Bonjour, messieurs-dames!
Hellos and goodbyes, Addressing people

Language

bonjour
bonsoir
salut
enchanté(e)
au revoir
ciao
bonne nuit
bonne journée
bonne soirée

[A]
Introduction

As the class comes in, speak to them in French straight away, giving your name and saying hello as appropriate. Introduce the whole group in simple terms: *Et vous, comment vous appelez-vous?* Introduce *répéter* and various items of classroom language such as, *encore, vous pouvez répéter, s'il vous plaît, c'est bien, bravo!* This will set the tone (using the target language) from the outset.

[B] ((•))
Activity 1

Student Book p.10
Explain to the students which greetings are appropriate in the given circumstances. OHP cues of *bonne nuit, au revoir* can help their responses. They can then do Activity 1 as set. Check student answers, then play the tape again, having students imitate what they hear.

[C]
Activity 2   Allez-y!

Student Book p.10
Do the activity as set and check the answers. Then use the letters a–f as a prompt to cue the French responses. Write the letters on the board as you say them in French as this will help when you come to the French alphabet later.

T: E.
S: Bonne nuit!

De A à Z
Spelling with the French alphabet

[A]
Introduction

Ask students to spell their name in English. As they do so, translate the letters into French and note them on the board. Continue with a variety of names until students are familiar with the sounds. Then go through the notes given on p.11 and listen to the tape with the students.

[B] ((•))
Activity 1

Student Book p.11
Do the activity as set and then ask the students to spell the French names, in random order. Use the question, *Ça s'écrit comment?* each time. Teach the question and have the students practise it.

[C] ((•))
Activities 2 and 3   Allez-y!

Student Book p.11
These activities can now be done. If students need further practice in the French alphabet they can try to remember names of people in the class and spell them. The person who is spelled out, must then spell another class member and so on.

Un café, s'il vous plaît!
Asking for things

Language

oui
non
c'est là-bas
s'il vous plaît
une gare
une voie
un café
un thé
une bière
un coca
un jus de fruit

un vin rouge
bonne idée!

excusez-moi, monsieur
pardon
mademoiselle, s'il vous plaît

le taxi, la gare
un café, une bière
des cafés, des bières

[A]
Activity 1

Student Book p.12
You can extend this activity by getting students to ask for some of the things they have mentioned in talking about the cartoon.

T: Vous commandez un vin rouge...
S: Un vin rouge, s'il vous plaît. ...

[B] ((*))
Activity 2

Student Book p.13
Collect pictures of the drinks mentioned and use the pictures to elicit the words from students. Have them add *s'il vous plaît*, and hand the corresponding picture to the student who asks for it. You may well need to explain the meaning of *croque-monsieur*.

[C]
Activity 3   Allez y!

Student Book p.13
Read through the *Mot à mot* on p.12 a couple of times for the students and then have them read the phrases. Get them to quiz each other in pairs on the vocabulary.

S1: Qu'est-ce que c'est en anglais, un coca?
S2: 'Coca Cola'. Comment dit-on en français, 'good idea'?
S1: Bonne idée. ...

Ask them to close their books and try to **remember** the phrases. They can now perform dialogues with the class as a whole, or in pairs, in the café.

Un, deux, trois...
Numbers up to 20

[A] ((*))
Introduction

Student Book p.13
Once students have listened to the tape and begun to pronounce the numbers with some confidence, write some up randomly on the board. Say some aloud and have the students write them down (as figures).

[B] ((*))
Activity 1

Student Book p.13
Do this activity and check the answers students have written. They can then perfom the dialogue first with, then without, the text.

[C] ((*))
Activity 2

Student Book p.13
Once students have completed the activity to fill in the prices, they can play the part of the customer asking prices and the waitress replying.

[D]
Play with numbers

Give students an example sequence of numbers: *trois, six, neuf...* and write it on the board. Ask them to continue it, then say something such as, *OK, à vous d'inventer une séquence...* indicating that they should note one down, ready to announce to the group. The rest of the class must then continue the sequence.

[E]
Points de repère

Student Book p.13
Encourage students to check what they have learned in this unit by testing each other in pairs. They can then record their achievements by filling in the grid provided.

UNITÉ 1 PRÉSENTATIONS

Je m'appelle Corinne
Introducing yourself, Numbers from 20 to 70

Language

un agent des postes
un(e) architecte
un(e) étudiant(e)
un(e) garagiste
un(e) journaliste
une mère au foyer
un professeur
un(e) secrétaire
mon prénom
un nom de famille
Je suis au chômage
Je suis retraité(e)
Qu'est-ce que vous faites comme métier?

je m'appelle
j'ai 33 ans
je suis journaliste
Comment vous appelez-vous?
Vous vous appelez comment?
Quel âge avez-vous? Vous avez quel âge?

[A]
Introduction to the unit

You may already know what some of the group members do for a living and you can now use that information for conversations.

T: Alors, vous vous appelez Eric. Oui? Et vous êtes plombier? Moi, je suis professeur de français... Et vous, Deborah, vous êtes journaliste? Oui? Moi, je suis professeur de français.

From your conversations list all words for jobs on the board/OHP.

[B]
Practice of names

Early in the course, you can help students 'get their mouths round' words in the following way: choose a range of names from those given in *Culturoscope* on p.15 and write them in a list:

1 Jean	6 Pascal
2 Elodie	7 Petit
3 Julien	8 Durand
4 Madeleine	9 Moreau
5 Thomas	10 Yvonne

When you say a number between one and ten, students say the corresponding name. Or, you (or other students) say a name and students say the corresponding number. This is an economical way of practising words intensively and reduces the amount of correction needed later.

[C]
Introduction of numbers 20 to 70

Students will need these for talking about ages in this unit. After initial presentation and repetition, numbers can be practised by quick dictation (you say *cinquante-cinq, soixante, soixante-sept* and students write 55, 60, 67), or by using a noughts and crosses frame (see Introduction p.000).

[D] ((•))
Dialogue   Je m'appelle Corinne Baudelot
Student Book p.14

Play the tape and help students to pick out forenames, surnames, ages and jobs. These could be entered on to a simple grid with four headings:

Prénom	Nom de famille	Age	Travail

Spell out, or ask the class to spell out, in French some of the names on the grid to reinforce the use of the alphabet. Having gathered the information from the tape, concentrate on the question forms, ensuring that students see that the two forms – *Comment vous appelez-vous?/Vous vous appelez comment?* – are interchangeable in an informal situation.

[E] ((•))
Activity 1

Student Book p.15
Do the first activity using the tape while students tick the numbers they hear. Then get the students to say one each of the remaining numbers until all the squares are ticked.

[F] ((•))
Activity 2

Student Book p.15
This is a good point at which to do this listening
activity in which students match people's names and
jobs.

[G]
Comment vous appelez-vous? Quel est votre métier?

Show the students the abbreviations you will use to
recall the words for jobs (*sec = secrétaire, arch =
architecte*). You could put these abbreviations on a set
of flashcards and add to them as others occur later in
the course for revision.

[H]
Choice Framework 1.1 p.115

Students need as much practice in asking questions as
in providing answers, e.g. by having prompts such as
Nom? Travail? on the board/OHP. Indicate which
question you want them to ask by pointing at the
prompt, answering the questions yourself with a
variety of information taken from the unit – *Je suis
architecte, je m'appelle Corinne Baudelot...*

Using Choice Framework 1.1 students choose and
note on a slip of paper a forename, a surname, an age
and a job from each column. Invite volunteers to ask a
question – perhaps by pointing at the prompt word at
the top of a column, or simply by saying: *Alors, qui va
poser une question?* Student A asks a classmate, who
responds with the information noted on her/his slip of
paper.

A: *Comment vous appelez-vous?*
B: *(Je m'appelle) Elodie Thomas.*
A: *Et quel est votre métier?*
B: *(Je suis) étudiante.*
A: *Et vous avez quel âge?*
B: *(J'ai) trente ans.*

B: *Qu'est-ce que vous faites comme métier?*
A: *(Je suis) garagiste.*
B: *Et vous vous appelez comment?*
A: *(Je m'appelle) Madeleine Moreau.*
B: *Quel âge avez-vous?*
A: *(J'ai) cinquante ans.*

Note that students do not need to repeat the verb from
the question in their answer. If you want students to
use full sentences, give a more general prompt: *Alors,
vous vous présentez, s'il vous plaît?* This will elicit a
response such as: *Eh bien, je m'appelle Madeleine
Moreau. J'ai cinquante ans. Je suis garagiste.*

[I]
Activity 3   Vous y êtes?

Student Book p.15
Ask students to say the eight phrases in French. Check
their answers. Now give them one key word only for
each of the phrases on OHP/board and ask them if
they can remember the answer. In this way *trente-
deux* prompts *j'ai trente-deux ans*, and *Geo Lép*
prompts *je m'appelle Georges Lépine.*

This is another way to practise the target items, but
the challenge/motivation is different.

[J]
Activity 5   Et vous?

Student Book p.15
Students can now work in pairs, talking about
themselves. They should note the information they
gather. They may well need to ask their partner(s) to
repeat things, so make sure that they have heard you
say, *Vous pouvez répéter, s'il vous plaît?* or an
equivalent. Students can then circulate among the
whole group, getting to know as many people as they
can.

J'habite en France
Saying where you live

Language

l'Afrique du Nord(f)
l'Allemagne (f)
l'Angleterre (f)
les Antilles (f)
l'Australie (f)
la Belgique
l'Ecosse (f)
l'Espagne (f)
les Etats-Unis (m)
la Grande-Bretagne
l'Irlande (f)
l'Italie (f)
les Pays-Bas (m)
le pays de Galles
le Royaume-Uni
la Suède
la Suisse
la région
toujours
maintenant
le sud de

j'habite en Belgique, au Canada, aux Etats-Unis
j'habite (à)12 Marseille

je suis de La Rochelle

[A] 🔊
Dialogue   *Où habitez-vous?*

Student Book p.16

Play the tape bit by bit, explaining any unfamiliar language. This can be done in French with sketches such as points of the compass for *le sud de l'Espagne*. Explain that many French people, when asked their name, will give their surname first, as Gabriel Persyn does. When students understand the model dialogues, they can practise the question forms: *Où habitez-vous? Vous habitez où? Vous êtes de la région?* Their answers can then refer to themselves: *Je suis de York. J'habite maintenant au sud de l'Angleterre...*

With an OHP it is useful to have a transparency with a number of speech bubbles (there is one on p.114). You can place notes or symbols in a speech bubble to act as a prompt for students to recall what that person is saying:

S1: *Vous êtes de la région?*
S2: *Non, je suis d'Oxford. Et vous habitez où?*
S1: *J'habite maintenant dans le sud de la France.*

[B] 🔊
Activity 1

Student Book p.16

Students can now listen to six people saying where they live and tick the cities they mention.

[C]
Activity 2   *Vous y êtes?*

Student Book p.16

These phrases should be easy for students to translate, though they may well need help with the elision of *e* before *Orléans*, by analogy with *je suis d'Hesdin* in the model dialogue.

[D]
Activity 3   *Allez-y!*

Student Book p.17

Students can do the activity by imagining they live in the cities shown. You can then extend this activity by asking them to recall the statements afterwards, using the photo as a prompt.

[E]
Activity 4   *Et vous?*

Student Book p.17

This can be done as a paired activity in class, using either people's real identities or by inviting them to invent a name, a country and a city, town or village. Practise the questions just once more before they work in pairs: *Vous vous appelez comment? Vous habitez où? Vous êtes de la région?* Alternatively, students could give short presentations: *Je m'appelle Pierre Blanc. Je suis de Montréal. J'habite maintenant à Londres.*

Je suis français – Je suis française
Giving your nationality

Language

Vous êtes né(e)...?
Vous êtes de quelle nationalité?
bien sûr
donc
et
moi-même
allemand(e)
américain(e)
anglais(e)
australien(ne)
belge
britannique
écossais(e)
espagnol(e)
français(e)
gallois(e)
iranien(ne)
irlandais(e)
italien(ne)
japonais(e)
marocain(e)n
suédois(e)

je suis français/française
je suis né(e) à...
je suis né(e) en France, au Japon, aux Etats-Unis
je suis de nationalité française/d'origine italienne
Vous êtes né(e)...?
Vous êtes de quelle nationalité?

[A]
Spelling

Use the interview from p.18 with Hassan Zouazou as a base for revising the French alphabet. As well as writing the letters on the board, and saying them in alphabetical order, ask students to spell out some of the names which they have already used (*Jean,*

Moreau, Petit) as well as their own surnames.

[B] ((•))
Activity 1

Student Book p.18
Read the given statements and let students do this as a reading exercise first, before they listen to the tape to check their answers. The activity can be extended if students read aloud what they have heard and noted.

[C]
Activity 2   Vous y êtes?

Student Book p.19
Point out the analogy between *je suis* + nationality and *je suis* + occupation. Students might want to put an indefinite article before the occupation – don't let them!

[D]
Activity 3   Allez-y!

Student Book p.19
This activity can be done in writing or orally in class. If done orally, it can easily be extended if students are invited to supply further sentences using places not covered in the exercise: *Je suis née à Cardiff. Je suis né à Tokyo.*

[E] ((•))
Activity 4

Student Book p.19
Play the conversations several times. With their books closed, students note down in French the nationalities and countries they hear. Ask them to report back what they have noted. Students can go back and check the spellings later. This will help the class associate the sound with the written form of the word. Correcting their work will reinforce the spelling.

[F] ((•))
Activity 5   Allez-y!

Student Book p.19
Let the students hear the dialogue in its full form once or twice – they can decide for themselves when they are ready to provide the answers, then the questions. The taped version for students to supply the missing information has pauses after the questions to give them time to respond. The version in which students must supply the questions has prompts in English.

[G] ((•))
Activity 6   Et vous?

Student Book p.19
This pulls together the unit as a whole. It could be prepared by using speech bubbles – put question

prompts one by one in one set of bubbles and notes like those given below in another, to practise the kind of dialogues students will later perform with the cue cards.

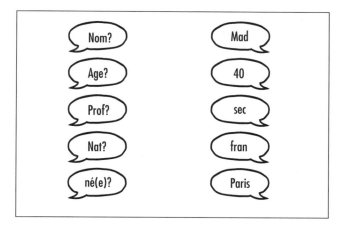

To practise some of the adjectives, adjectival agreements and names of countries, use a speech bubble transparency. For a male speaker, put the word *Montréal* in the bubble. Students supply: *Je suis de Montréal.* Show that, *Ah, vous êtes canadien?* is one possible response, then provide practice along the following lines:

Montréal

T: *Je suis de Montréal.*
T/S: *Ah, vous êtes canadien?*
T/S: *Oui.*

T: *Je suis de Toronto.*
S: *Ah, vous êtes canadienne?*
T: *Oui.*

Toronto

S1: *Je suis de Bristol.*
S2: *Ah, vous êtes anglaise? ...*

[H]
A Capital Game

Agree that all speakers live in the capital of their country. First you, then student volunteers, can give their nationality and others name their city.

T: Je suis anglaise.
S1: Vous habitez Londres?
T: Oui, (bien sûr).
S1: Je suis australienne.
S2: Vous habitez Canberra?
S1: Oui, (bien sûr).

The intention is not to test geographical knowledge but the constraint of using only capital cities adds an extra challenge.

[I]
Cue Cards 1.2 p.115

The set of cue cards provides further practice of the language students have learned in this unit. The notes about their assumed identity can serve as prompts for the necessary questions. Students will need to be warned that the actual question forms are not given.

Ça va?
Asking people if they're OK

[A]
Introduction of ça va?

Explain the different uses of *ça va?* as set out in the Student Book on p.20

[B] ⸨⸩
Activity 1

Student Book p.20
Play the tape and ask students to write the correct snatch of conversation for each frame of the cartoon. Check the answers by playing the tape a second time.

[C]
Points de repère

Student Book p.21
Encourage students to check what they have learned in this unit by testing each other in pairs. They can then record their achievements by filling in the grid provided.

UNITÉ 2 FAMILLE

Je suis célibataire
Talking about your marital status

Language

ami(e)
avec
célibataire
divorcé(e)
une femme
un mari
marié(e)
un médecin généraliste
quelqu'un
séparé(e)
seul
un veuf
une veuve
je ne suis pas (receptive)

s'appeler – il/elle s'appelle
comment s'appelle-t-il/elle?
être – il/elle est
mon, ma, mes
vivre, je vis

[A] ((·))
Dialogue   Vous êtes mariée?

Student Book p.24
Play the tape bit by bit using it for repetition in small sections from which you can encourage the class to ask and answer questions (i.e. the first eight lines). Then move on to the next four lines explaining language as necessary. Much of this can be done in French.

T: *Sarah est célibataire. Elle n'est pas mariée. Elle est célibataire. John est célibataire aussi. Il n'est pas...?*
S: *Marié.*
T: *Oui. Il est donc...?*

Students can note the questions from the interviews as they will be needed for the task in [D] below.

[B]
Il /Elle s'appelle... Il/Elle est...

Draw three or four pin figures on the OHP/board (or alternatively use photos or pictures from magazines) and give them names suggested by the students to introduce *il/elle s'appelle...*

T: *Comment s'appelle-t-il/elle? (Il/Elle s'appelle comment?)*
S: *Harry/Harriet.*
T: *Il/Elle est anglais(e), français(e), tunisien(ne)?*
S: *Irlandais(e).*

Add professions to the pin figures and ask the class to describe them. Encourage them then to create more for you to sketch on the OHP/board. This involves the use of *être* and *s'appeler*. Ask students to quiz each other about the people.

S1: *Harriet, elle est française?*
S2: *Non, elle est irlandaise. Elle est professeur?*

[C]
Extending to je

Add *marié(e), célibataire, séparé(e), divorcé(e)* to the profiles and using the *il/elle* forms continue practising with the students. Add *elle vit avec.../seul(e)*. This can be done by using the symbol of a house with names next to it:

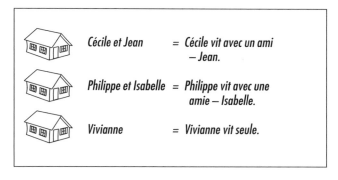

Cécile et Jean	= *Cécile vit avec un ami – Jean.*
Philippe et Isabelle	= *Philippe vit avec une amie – Isabelle.*
Vivianne	= *Vivianne vit seule.*

To move into the first person, describe yourself, or put speech bubbles around the profiles with the words you have put on the OHP/board. The students already know *je suis* and *je m'appelle*. The new form is *je vis*.

[D]
Making up profiles using all the language

Encourage students to create profiles using consistent symbols and abbreviations which you have agreed with the class. The profiles may be real or not:

Marie; prof; cél;

Marc; div; suisse; méc

T/S: *Je m'appelle Marie. Je suis professeur. Je suis*

célibataire et je vis avec un ami. Il s'appelle Marc. Il est suisse et il est mécanicien. Il est divorcé.

In groups of two or four ask them to talk about their profiles while the other students note the details. Change the groups so that students can find out further details from a new partner. When they have done this they will have both answered and asked the relevant questions. The students now report back introducing one person to the group: *C'est Marie. Elle est professeur...*

[E]
Mon, ma

At this stage introduce *ami(e)* and *femme. Mari* has been introduced in the first dialogue of the unit and can be used to introduce the new language using the relationships of the class members. Write *ma femme, mon ami, mon amie, mon mari*, and practise them either as reality or for invented people.

T: Qui est marié? Ah, Stephen. Votre femme, comment s'appelle-t-elle?
S1: Paula.
T: Merci. Alors, moi, je vis avec **mon** *mari/ami. Mon mari/ami s'appelle Michael et la femme de Stephen s'appelle Paula. Et vous autres? (prompt) Je vis avec mon ami/ma...*
S2: Je vis avec mon mari. Il s'appelle Peter.
S3: Mon amie s'appelle Julie.

You may prefer not to use *la femme de/le mari de... s'appelle...* because *le* and *la* have not yet been introduced, however the class could understand these receptively at this stage. You will need to be careful about the responses so that students do not get into *je vis avec elle/lui*, though this is quite easy to teach. *Mon, ma* and *mes* can be more intensively practised when more has been covered in the unit.

[F] ((•))
Activity 1

Student Book p.25
This tape can be used in a variety of ways in class.
Students can:
* make notes during several listenings and then
* question each other about them
* interview each other as a role play
* write up an account for homework.

[G]
Activity 2   Vous y êtes?
Activity 3   Allez-y!

Student Book p.25
These activities can be done in small groups or pairs and then gone over in the whole class. By doing the

activities in small groups, students obtain more intensive language practice.

[H] ((•))
Activity 4   Et vous?

Student Book p.25
This can be developed as in [F] above and then students can interview each other about themselves.

[I]
Cue Cards 2.1 p.116

Students can now use the cue cards which contain a range of details. They work in pairs exchanging information as though they were the people on the cards.

J'ai quatre enfants
Talking about your children

Language

l'aîné(e)
aussi
un collège
le dernier
la dernière
des
le/la deuxième
une école
une école maternelle
une école primaire
également
un enfant
ensuite
un(e) étudiant(e)
une fille
un fils
un garçon
en gestion
un lycée
une maison
un mois
qui
votre

Il/elle s'appelle comment?
Qu'est-ce qu'il/elle fait?
Quel âge a...?
j'ai + substantive
je n'ai pas de...
il/elle a... ans
à la, au

[A] ((·))
Dialogue   Vous êtes marié?

Student Book p.26
Students will understand most of this dialogue, and from it you can derive language for them to respond to your questions about whether they have children: *J'ai... enfant(s)/fille(s)/garçon(s)*. Teach *je n'ai pas d'enfants* as it arises in class. Encourage students to ask each other whether they have children. You could hand out slips of paper having written on a number, i.e. 0, 1, 3, or words *1 garçon(s)*, and ask students to pretend they have that number of children. They can invent names.

[B] ((·))
Activity 2

Student Book p.27
Using the dialogue for comprehension, you will be able to extend the students' vocabulary. The French first names give you a good opportunity to practise spelling in French with the class.

For further practice of *son/sa/ses* draw a family tree of the Jays on the board/OHP using pin figures. Label Christine Jay. Pointing at the first child, ask: *Qui est-ce?* Students answer: *C'est Hubert, son fils.* Continue asking questions until all the children and M. Jay are in the right place.

[C]
Extending the language – âge, fils, fille, être au lycée

Build on the language of the previous section. You will need to teach the following questions, the first of which is in Jean-Paul Jasserand's interview at the beginning of this section: *Ils/Elles s'appellent comment? Comment s'appellent-ils/elles? Quel âge ont-ils/elles?* There is no need to go into the grammar (*ils -ent*) as it comes in the next section. Create people and establish children, ages and names with the class. They will therefore hear the two questions given above straight away. You will need to explain that the use of *ils* includes masculine and feminine.

Establish *fils* and *fille – Maurice a un fils...* You can create two or three more families. This will require the

use of *ils ont des enfants* if you create a couple with children. Establish also what they do: *Son fils est soldat à Metz. Sa fille Chantale est élève au lycée, et sa fille Josée est élève au collège.*

Encourage the class to describe them and to ask questions: *X a des enfants?/X a combien d'enfants? Comment s'appellent-ils/elles? X, quel âge a-t-il/elle? Que fait-il/elle/Guy (son fils)?* You may wish to write the facts beneath the family as shown above, and include other language (*école primaire, maternelle*) under the other families you have created. Also practise talking about children of a few months old: *il a six mois.*

[D]
Practising the language

Students are now in a position to seek and give information on family size and composition, ages, what people do and where they work. They can move around the class and ask questions either referring to themselves or to invented identities. The task is therefore to ask all they can think of from this unit. Students can be asked to note their findings and report back. They would need to be able to use *son, sa, ses* to do this fully but it can be avoided: *Il a deux enfants, Max a treize ans et Anne a cinq ans.*

[E]
Further practice of mon, ma, mes

To practise *mon, ma* and *mes* as a specific exercise, put several families on the OHP/board as shown below and ask students to make statements for other students to identify who is speaking.

S1: Mon mari a quarante-six ans.
S2: C'est Yvonne. (Yvonne est sa femme.)
T: Oui. Quelqu'un d'autre?
S3: Mes fils ont deux ans et seize mois...

[F] ((•))
Activity 3   Allez-y!
Activity 4   Et vous?

Student Book p.27
These activities can be done in pairs or small groups.

Je vous présente ma famille
Describing your family

Language

le cousin
la cousine
le demi-frère
la demi-sœur
le frère
la grand-mère
les grands-parents
le grand-père
la grand-mère
la mère
le neveu
la nièce
l'oncle
les parents
le père
la sœur
la tante

avoir – a/ont
être – est/sont – né(e)s
vivre – vit/vivent

[A] ((•))
Dialogue   Vous vous appelez comment?

Student Book p.28
There is a certain amount of information that you can ask students for from the tape which also provides a model for asking when and where someone was born. New language includes *née en 68* and *le 10 août*. Extend this by talking about yourself: *J'habite à (Londres), mais je suis né(e) à Newcastle* or *en France* and then ask students where they live and were born. You need to put both parts of the question to enable the students to use *naître* naturally in their answers: *J'habite..., mais je suis né(e)...*

[B] ((•))
Activity 1

Student Book p.28
The extended family can be introduced by using the tapes from Activities 1 and 2. Activity 1 introduces

père and *mère* and from this you can ask about the parents of class members. You will probably need to extend the range of numbers beyond 70 in order to do this.

[C] ((•))
Activity 2

Student Book p.28
Extend the language by using this dialogue. Note the new words for relatives and ask about the students' families, their ages and where they live. The number of grandparents available to talk about will depend on the age of the class and you will need to ask questions like: *Qui a un grand-père?* You can get students to use these words however by asking questions as outlined below which have two elements to them.

T: John. Vous avez des grands-parents et des cousins/oncles/tantes?
J: J'ai trois cousins et une cousine.

Almost certainly you will need to teach *mort(e)*, and if you want to use the imperfect tense just point it out and put it on the board/OHP: *Votre mère a (avait) combien de frères?*

[D] ((•))
Activity 3

Student Book p.29
This dialogue can be helpful in extending the range of language by question and answer as you go through it after doing the true/false activity in the Student Book.

[E]
Activity 5   Allez-y!
Activity 6   Et vous?

Student Book p.29
Students can work together on both of these activities. They can draw imaginary family trees for each other to describe in addition to doing Activity 6.

[F]
Cue Cards 2.2 p.116
Worksheet 2.3 p.116

These cue cards provide a simple whole class activity. Extended families of four people are shown on the cards. Each family is divided between four cards, on each of which is the name of one family member. Distribute the cards among the class. Each student has Worksheet 2.3 with the four names on and the number of people in that family. Students move about asking other students for details of the four families. When they have completed the worksheet, they have finished. The language needed is outlined below.

S1: La famille d'André, s'il vous plaît./Vous avez la famille d'André?/de Sylvie?/de Raoul?/de Sandrine?
S2: Oui. Il a un frère. Il a dix-neuf ans. Et un neveu. Il a un mois.
S1 writes down frère 19 ans, neveu 1 mois.

Tu t'appelles comment?
Using the right form of address

Language

des animaux
un(e) chien(ne)
un furet
je ne suis pas
ton, ta, tes
votre, vos

tu/vous + être, avoir, habiter, appeler
s'il vous/te plaît

[A]

In this block students have the opportunity to use the two forms of address, *vous* and *tu*. They have already come across a number of the forms: *Vous avez, vous habitez/vivez, vous vous appelez, votre fils a quel âge?*

[B] ((•))
Dialogue   Bonjour

Student Book p.30
Play the tape to introduce the familiar form. The dialogue is suitable for modelling and so repetition and then re-enactment could be used. A very simple cue card activity (explained in [D] below) practises this and includes nationality. Before doing the cue card activity you may like to do Activities 2 and 3 with the class using the tape as suggested on p.18 and also as suggested in the Introduction.

[C]
Activity 4   Allez-y!

Student Book p.31
After doing the activity in the Student Book, students can be asked to put the following questions either in the familiar or polite forms: *1. Tu es née à Paris?*
2. Vous avez des enfants? 3. Vous habitez en France?
4. Quel âge as-tu? 5. Comment s'appelle votre sœur?
6. Vos enfants, quel âge ont-ils? 7. Comment s'appellent tes parents? 8. C'est votre chien?

[D]
Cue Cards 2.4 p.117

Students use the cards in the same way as in the taped interview in [B]. When they have done one card they take another. Students will need to ask how to spell certain names. Explain the conventions to the class that the tutor would normally use the *vous* form with students, as you have been doing. In order to give them practice they need to role play a more familiar relationship with you and to role play talking to children. Some members of the class are quite likely to know each other well enough to use the *tu* form. Revise some of the language students already know using the *tu* form (name, age, family) and the ideas suggested in the relevant sections. To focus attention, put the key words that may be appropriate to a conversation on the board/OHP:

> *domicile;*
>
> *famille – frère, sœur, père, mère (noms, âges);*
>
> *métiers des parents;*
>
> *être à l'école/au collège/lycée/à la maison*

The range would be greater when talking with an adult: *femme, mari, enfants.* For a way of practising *ton, ta, tes* students could use the noughts and crosses game (see Introduction).

Comptez jusqu'à cent!
Numbers from 70–100

[A] ((•))
Numbers

Student Book p.32
Use the tape to introduce the new numbers giving students opportunity to repeat them several times.

[B]

Activities for learning and practising numbers

Use the activities suggested in the Student Book for practice and reinforcement. In learning and practising numbers it is helpful to many students to do this by direct perception of the figure rather than by translation or adding and subtracting numbers. Some ways of practising numbers are given below.

* Noughts and crosses game (see Introduction).
* Two or three students play with two dice. They say a number from the faces thrown. For example, a four and a three could be 43 or 34. If students wish, they can keep score of, say, five throws to see who gets the highest score.

[C] ((•))
Choice Framework 2.5 p.117

This framework can now be used to revise and practise the language of Units 1 and 2. The classroom practice can be led by you, done as pairwork or given as a written homework. See the Introduction for further suggestions about how to use frameworks. From this grid, students can make as many conversations as they wish to.

S1: *Vous habitez où?*
S2: *A Paris. Et vous?*
S1: *A Grenoble. Je suis mécanicien. Et vous, que faites-vous?*
S2: *Je suis architecte.*
S1: *Vous êtes français?*
S2: *Oui. Et vous?*
S1: *Je suis belge. Vous êtes marié(e)?/Vous avez des enfants?/Vous avez de la famille?*
S2: *Je suis divorcé. J'ai deux filles.*

[D]
Points de repère

Student Book p.33
Encourage students to check what they have learned in this unit by testing each other in pairs. They can then record their achievements by filling in the grid provided.

UNITÉ 3 PROFESSIONS

Je travaille dans une banque
Saying where you work and whether you like your job

Language

un ingénieur
une banque
une bibliothèque
un bureau
c'est-à-dire
un(e) comptable
enseigner
un étranger
les financements d'entreprise
français langue étrangère
grand(e)
un grand magasin
un hôpital
un infirmier/une infirmière
un(e) mécanicien(ne)
j'ai été militaire
une langue
un magasin
maintenant
plusieurs
une usine
un vendeur/une vendeuse

Où travaillez-vous? Vous travaillez où?
je travaille dans un(e)...
... à la Bibliothèque Nationale
... pour un journal
... chez Citroën
... comme ingénieur
je suis secrétaire
je m'occupe de...
Ça vous plaît?
oui, ça me plaît beaucoup
non, ça ne me plaît pas
c'est intéressant, ennuyeux, fatigant
j'aime mon travail

[A] ((·))
Dialogue   *Quelle est votre profession?*
Student Book p.36
Revise questions asking about what people do for a living from Units 1 and 2 using the vocabulary already known. Add the new vocabulary by using the recorded interviews and making notes to act as an

aide-memoire. These can be added to the set of flashcard symbols started in Unit 1.

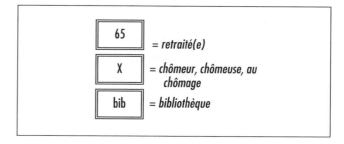

Students should not feel that they need to remember all the details in these interviews and the emphasis should be on the new professions, places of work and on the questions: *Quelle est votre profession? Qu'est-ce que vous faites? Ça vous plaît comme travail?*

[B]
Identities

At this stage, or later, describe a number of people in terms of where they live/work and other known details using the language from Units 1 and 2. Students guess the identities.

T: *Il est français. Il travaille à l'Elysée.*
Il est socialiste. Il est anglais. Il travaille à Londres, et il habite au 10, Downing Street.
Elle est anglaise. Elle habite Londres et elle est mariée. Elle travaille dans un bureau à Covent Garden (this is one of the students).

Use people who are in the news at the moment or personalities from TV, sport, politics and the music world.

[C]
Il travaille où/chez qui?

A range of answers to these questions can be presented through quick sketches of names, jobs, places, etc. labelled with names or symbols which are familiar to students.

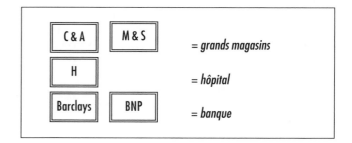

3 23

S/T: *Georges Blanc est médecin. Il travaille dans un hôpital (à Paris). Madeleine Blanc est bibliothécaire. Elle travaille dans une bibliothèque (à Marseille). Elle est divorcée ...*

[D]
Ça vous plaît comme travail?
Oui, ça me plaît beaucoup

Simple symbols for liking/disliking (hearts/ticks and crosses) will help students understand and then recall the question and answer sequence. These can be added to the details on the board/OHP and used as the stimulus for dialogues.

T: *Eric, vous êtes plombier. Ça vous plaît comme travail?*
E: *Oui, ça me plaît beaucoup.*
T: *Imaginez que vous êtes Madeleine.* (see above)

Question? (pointing to symbol for liking)
Vous aimez votre travail?
E: *Oui, ça me plaît beaucoup. / Non, ça ne me plaît pas.*

[E] ((•))
Activity 1

Student Book p.37
Play the recording and ask students to indicate after the first example which English sentence it refers to. At the end, students could use the details given in English as a prompt to recall the French sentences.

[F]
Activity 2   Worksheet 3.1 p.118

Student Book p.37
Having practised the patterns (*à, chez, comme, dans*), you could set the gap-filling activity as part of the homework. If you do Activity 2 in class, ask students to complete Worksheet 3.1 for homework. This gives a number of sentences on the same pattern, the first few in gapped form and the others more open-ended.

[G] ((•))
Activity 4

Student Book p.37
Read the passage on Chantal Decourt aloud, ensuring that students understand it by asking questions in French: *Quelle est sa profession?* Then play the tape for students to tell you in French what the two factual errors are. You may wish to give students further chances to hear some of the vocabulary given on the tape and in the paragraph by saying some sentences aloud and asking students to note the information and then feed it back.

T: *Monsieur Mitsumori est japonais. Il habite Tokyo et il travaille chez Nissan. Il est comptable.*
(students note: *M. Mitsumori; jap; Tok; compt*)
Madame McDonald est bibliothécaire. Elle travaille à Edimbourg.
(note: *Mme McD; bib; Edim*)
Madame Robinson est anglaise. Elle est professeur d'anglais langue étrangère, à Brighton. Elle est mariée, et elle a deux enfants.
(note: *Mme Rob; ang; prof ang; Brighton; mar; 2 enfs*)

[H]
Activity 5   Et vous?

Student Book p.37
This can be done as a pairwork exercise. Students need only a reminder of the questions they might ask: *Travail? Où?* Alternatively, they might make small presentations to the whole class, prompted by you: *Alors, Margaret, parlez-nous un peu de votre travail...*

Je travaille de neuf heures à midi
Times and working hours

Language

aux alentours de
après
l'après-midi
entre
en général
une heure
un horaire
une hôtesse d'accueil
j'ai un élevage de chats
un jour
tous les jours
midi
minuit
parfois
le matin
par semaine
le soir
jusqu'à
surtout

Quelle heure est-il? Il est quelle heure?
il est une heure, deux heures
il est une heure cinq, dix, et quart, vingt, vingt-cinq
il est une heure moins cinq, dix, le quart, vingt, vingt-cinq
je commence à neuf heures
je termine à cinq heures
je travaille de... à (jusqu'à) ...heures
huit heures par jour
quarante heures par semaine

[A]
Telling the time

Look at the clocks on p.39. Practise the relevant numbers quickly before going on to telling the time, perhaps with a noughts and crosses frame, or by having students count in twos or threes (*deux, quatre, six... / trois, six, neuf, douze...*). Say some times of day including *du matin, de l'après-midi, du soir*, and note them on the board:

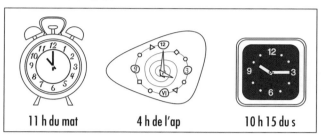

| 11 h du mat | 4 h de l'ap | 10 h 15 du s |

[B] ((·))
Activity 1

Student Book p.39
Play the tape and ask students to identify the times mentioned. Do them one at a time. Students could attempt to repeat the times with the intonation of the speaker.

[C]
Activity 3

Student Book p.39
Times round the world can be practised easily if you provide a table like this on the board/OHP:

NEW YORK	LONDRES	MOSCOU	HONG-KONG	SYDNEY
–6	0	+3	+7	+12

You can then ask: *Il est trois heures du matin à Londres: quelle heure est-il à Moscou? Et à New York?* Or using language taught in earlier units students choose one of the places from the table and volunteer: *A Londres, il est midi. Chez moi, il est minuit* and others deduce: *Vous habitez Sydney.*

[D] ((·))
Activities 4 and 5

Student Book p.39
Play the tape a bit at a time, giving students time to find the statements they need to ascribe to speakers, and for Activity 5, to write in the missing words. For further practice in talking about working hours, draw a time line on the board/OHP:

	6 7 8 9 10 11 12 13 14 15 16 17 18 19 20 21
Françoise	
Virginie	
Frank	

It is easy to indicate when the speakers start and finish their work by using an arrow from starting point to finishing point beside each person's name. Mark on the time line the information given in Activity 5, then give other examples for students to practise. If you put the time line on OHP, an overlay can be used for the arrows; this will mean that you don't waste time having to rub things out! Students then read back the information given on the time line: *Monsieur Blanc travaille de huit heures à dix-sept heures. Madame Blanc travaille de quatorze heures à vingt et une heures.*

[E]
Choice Framework 3.2 p.118

Students are given the opportunity here to put the questions they will need for communicative practice in work routines: *Qu'est-ce que vous faites dans la vie? Quelle est votre profession? Vous travaillez où? Vous commencez à quelle heure? Vous finissez/terminez à quelle heure? Vous travaillez de quelle heure à quelle heure? Vous aimez votre travail?*
You might like to add: *Vous travaillez combien d'heures par semaine? Vous avez combien de semaines de vacances?*

One student asks a question such as: *Comment vous appelez-vous?* Another student chooses any of the names from the first column; the next volunteer asks a question about a job, and a volunteer chooses from the second column, and so on. This activity is done with the whole class in preparation for the next activity.

[F] ((·))
Activity 6   Et vous?
Cue Cards 3.3 p.118

This work is to be done in pairs. Note the following:
* Questions are not provided on the cards; students use the information to prompt the questions they need.
* The information is not presented in the same order on all the cards, so that students can choose where to begin, and cannot answer their partner's questions mechanically from top to bottom of the card.
* Students are encouraged to use the words listed at the bottom where they can; this means they supply occasional pieces of information not given on the card: *Je travaille parfois jusqu'à vingt heures.*

3 25

* You might like to provide a blank grid on which students note the information they obtain. Have some of them report back to the whole group – this requires adaptation to third person forms and can allow longer utterances if you ask students a general question: *Parlez-moi de Gregory Harrison.*

Du lundi au vendredi
Days of the week, Frequency

Language

un boulanger-pâtissier
un traiteur
dimanche
lundi
mardi
mercredi
jeudi
vendredi
samedi
tous les jours
je ne travaille pas
je vais
j'y vais
ne jamais
à la piscine
repos
le soir
au théâtre

je vais au cinéma le dimanche matin
je ne travaille pas le mercredi
je ne vais jamais au théâtre
je vais très peu au cinéma
je vais très souvent au restaurant
je vais à la piscine trois fois par an

[A]
ne...pas/plus

New patterns are best presented by working with known vocabulary: *Je ne travaille pas* and later *je ne travaille plus.* Use this new pattern with the old material:

T: *Moi, je travaille ici à X, mais je n'habite pas à X. J'habite à Y. Je suis né à Paris, mais je n'habite plus Paris, j'habite Clermont Ferrand. Mon fils ne vit plus avec nous. Il habite à Z.*

Note that Activity 4 requires students to distinguish between *ne pas* and *ne plus.*

[B] ((•))
Dialogue   Vous vous appelez comment?

Student Book p.40
Use the model dialogues to introduce days of the week and the key questions: *Vous commencez à quelle heure le matin? Vous travaillez tous les jours de la semaine? Tu sors beaucoup?* Collect together the leisure activities mentioned in the recording and note them on the board/OHP or collect pictures from magazines for use as an aide-memoire:

th	= théâtre
pis	= piscine
amis	= chez mes amis
parents	= chez mes parents

Write up in a column expressions to do with frequency and combine them with the leisure pursuits: *souvent, très peu, jamais, une fois par semaine, le mercredi soir, le week-end...*

[C]
Practising days of the week

Like numbers, these are generally learned in sequence. It is useful to provide practice which helps each of them take on its independent meaning. Use them in contexts known to all.

T: *Le dimanche, est-ce que le supermarché Sainsbury est ouvert? Et Boots? Et vous, vous avez cours de français le samedi ou le mardi? Et votre fille, Jacqueline, elle va à l'école le mercredi? Et en France, à l'école primaire, il y a classe le mercredi?*

[D]
A time line

A time line with the seven days of the week can be used like the one for working hours. *Elle/Il travaille tous les jours de la semaine?* will require students to practise days of the week in context: *Non, elle travaille (surtout) le week-end; il travaille le lundi et le mardi; le mercredi, c'est repos.* Students can be invited to make up some people and their working hours, marked on the time line with an arrow or with ticks. They can then report back.

[E] ((•))
Activity 1

Student Book p.40
This recording should be straightforward, but students may need help with *je dîne chez eux.*

[F] (((•)))
Activity 3

Student Book p.41
Students may have difficulty with *quelques semaines*.

[G]
Activity 4   Et vous?

Student Book p.41
In addition to the examples, you can use the aide-memoire mentioned above to encourage students to ask questions: *Vous sortez souvent? Vous aimez le cinéma?* Answers can be either in the form: *J'y vais une fois par semaine* or simply, *oui, une fois par semaine*. The main focus is communication about frequency rather than teaching the pronoun *y*. Add some of the material from earlier in the unit to the questions you practise: *Vous allez souvent à la banque? Vous allez souvent à la bibliothèque?* Prompt words with question marks will allow you to get students to ask as well as to answer the questions.

Souvent?	Banque?	Bibliothèque?	Piscine?

These questions can be used for a guessing game. One student says, *moi, je sors...* and the others guess the place with questions such as: *Vous allez à la banque? Vous allez au restaurant? Vous allez à la piscine?* Practise the question forms needed for pair practice: *Vous travaillez tous les jours de la semaine? Vous allez souvent au restaurant/au cinéma/à la piscine? Vous sortez beaucoup?*

[H]
Worksheet 3.4 p.119

Students use the grid on the worksheet to interview classmates. They enter their own information in the first line and then carry out little interviews. The headings prompt the questions they have been learning. As students elicit information from others, they note it in the columns beneath their own entry. This can then be used for reporting back in the third person.

[I]
Interactive conversations

Students should be encouraged to make their exchanges more like real conversations as units progress. This can be done if you:
* Teach them a small number of ways of reacting – *ah, bon, vraiment! d'accord* – to show they have understood.
* Show them that questions do not always have to be put in the same way: *Moi, je suis bibliothécaire – et vous?* and that they are not always obliged to wait

to be asked questions, where, for instance, their information happens to coincide: *Vous travaillez tous les jours de la semaine? Oui. Moi aussi. Vous sortez beaucoup? Non, jamais. Moi non plus!*

24 heures de la vie d'une femme

Language

un(e) bénévole
une casquette
un chef de cabine
un courrier
les courses (f)
une durée
l'enfance
les garçons couchés
une hôtesse de l'air
UTA (Union de Transports Aériens)

This text is for gist reading. Students need to be reassured that they will be able to cope with the extended text.

It may be useful to take students through a number of useful strategies in reading longer texts:
* Headlines – point out that it is good to start by looking at the title and asking themselves what expectations this sets up, i.e. what is the article likely to include?
* Sub-headings (like the paragraph in capitals) – do they help to increase/modify our expectations?
* How many words do we already know?
* Which of the unfamiliar words look like their English equivalents?
* Are there any clues (in the linguistic context) which allow us to make intelligent guesses about meanings?

[A]
Activity 1

Student Book p.42
Students might underline the words they already know. Another useful step is to look for words which they do not know, but which look like their English equivalents (*cabine, gym, compagnie*).

[B]
Activity 2

Student Book p.42
These questions allow students to re-use language they have learned. The activity could be set as homework or done orally in class.

[C]
Activity 3

Student Book p.43
Ask the students to tell you exactly which word or words allowed them to locate the translations.

[D]
Activity 4

Student Book p.43
This could be set as homework. When checking answers, ask students to point out which parts of the text give each answer. As a last exercise, make an overhead transparency of the text, blanking out some of the expressions which you want students to remember for active use such as all expressions of frequency, *tous les matins*, and moments in the day, *en fin de matinée*.

The text adds to their store of adverbial phrases. You can profit from this by asking students to extend the range of questions they ask each other: *Qu'est-ce que vous faites après le dîner? Qu'est-ce que X fait tous les matins?*

[E]
Points de repère

Student Book p.43
Encourage students to check what they have learned in this unit by testing each other in pairs. They can then record their achievements by filling in the grid provided.

UNITÉ 4 VILLE OU CAMPAGNE

J'habite à Anvin
Saying where you live

Language

un appartement
en banlieue
au bord de la mer
à la campagne
au centre-ville
grand(e)
un(e) habitant(e)
un jardin
une maison
une montagne
le nord
on
petit(e)
situé(e)
un village
en ville
ça se trouve

verbs in -*er* ; all persons, present tense

[A]
Maison, appartement; je, il, elle vous, habiter Photocopy Master 4.1 p.119

Photocopy Master 4.1 includes *maison* and *appartement*. For presentation these can be photocopied on a transparency and cut up into individual squares. They can then be put together with place and people's names in various combinations so that the following is possible.

T: *J'habite une maison à (Manchester).* (placing picture on OHP/board) *Sandrine habite un appartement à Lyon. Marcel habite une maison à Montélimar. Alice habite un appartement à Rennes.*

Encourage contributions from students and put questions about the information. It will involve the use of *vous habitez* which you may initially have to give to the class.

T: *Qui habite à (Manchester)?*
S: *Vous.*
T: *Oui. Et à Lyon?*
S: *Sandrine.*

Develop this with more examples and then use a question containing a contrast. First present the question form: *Est-ce que...?*

T: *Marcel et Alice, est-ce qu'ils habitent un appartement?*
S: *Non. Marcel habite une maison, et Alice habite un appartement.*
T: *Et moi?*
S: *Vous habitez une maison.*
T: *Et vous?*

Ask students if they live in houses or flats and encourage them to ask each other. By now they will have used: *habiter – je, il, elle, vous.*

[B]
Vous habitez où? Où travaillez-vous? en banlieue, à la campagne, au centre-ville, dans un village/Manchester, habiter – ils/elles   Photocopy Master 4.1 p.119

Extend the above using Photocopy Master 4.1 in the same way to include the vocabulary given here. You may wish to look at the *Infolangue* on p.46, or leave this to the end of this piece of work. Present the language of saying where your house is and use questions as above. Encourage the students to ask the questions.

Introduce *travailler* and encourage its use by students. Use the plural form *ils/elles* in questions when asking about the people you have created on the board: *Jules et Claude, où est-ce qu'ils habitent?/Ils habitent où? Ils travaillent où? Ils travaillent à...?*

[C] ((•))
Dialogue   Vous habitez une maison ou un appartement?

Student Book p.46
Play the first tape extract and then ask questions about the content introducing *jardin, grand, petit.* Extend this to the class's houses: *Vous avez... Votre... Mon/Ma... est...* Use photos of houses from magazines for further language practice as to whether they have gardens, their size and where they are.

[D] ((•))
Dialogue   Et où habites-tu?

Student Book p.46
These recordings can be used for general

understanding and interviews can then be created from them. As students hear the recordings several times without using the book they can note down as much detail as possible, including the names of towns mentioned. They can then interview each other for language practice. Explain *département* and ask if the class can name any. The location of these departments can serve as a trailer for the next block.

[E]
Habiter   Worksheet 4.2 p.120

Look at the paradigm of the *-er* verb with students. Worksheet 4.2 can be used in class or, better, for homework. Discuss the use of *on* and the informal French use of *nous, on habite...*

[F]
Practising the language of the block
Choice Framework 4.3 p.121
Cue Cards 4.4 p.121

Students should be able to carry out a conversation much as follows using Choice Framework 4.3. When you feel that they have had sufficient practice as a whole class, you could use Cue Cards 4.4 for pairwork.

S1: Vous habitez un appartement ou une maison?
S2: Une maison. Et vous?
S1: J'habite un appartement à Nantes.
S2: Vous habitez où, à Nantes?
S1: J'habite au centre-ville. Et vous?
S2: J'habite dans un village mais je travaille à Brest, au centre-ville. Et vous? ...

[G] ((·))
Activity 1

Student Book p.47
Students can be encouraged to make notes from this tape when they have done the activity as suggested, and use them in class for narration practice: *Je m'appelle... et j'habite à... Mon frère habite à X au centre-ville.* They can also use the information they gather to create interviews with each other, adding to the information as they wish.

[H]
Activity 2

Student Book p.47
This can be done in class in pairs and then checked together.

[I]
Activity 3   Allez-y!

Student Book p.47

When you have done the activity in class, encourage students to alter it and develop different dialogues with each other following the same pattern.

[J] ((·))
Activity 4   Et vous?

Student Book p.47
Encourage students to work at this in pairs so that they can seek and give information with a number of students about where they live.

[K] ((·))
Homework   Worksheet 4.2 p.120
Choice Framework 4.3 p.121

The students could take Choice Framework 4.3 and write up a few portraits: *Marcel et Marc habitent à...* See also Worksheet 4.2 in which students are invited to write ten descriptive sentences. They can also use the framework to make up information on an imaginary self, which they use as the basis for interviews with each other. These could then be reported back to the whole class using the third person.

Anvin, c'est dans le nord de la France
Locating places

Language

l'est
le nord
le nord-est
le nord-ouest
l'ouest
le sud
le sud-est
le sud-ouest
C'est où?
Où est...?
à X kilomètres/minutes/heure(s) de
à côté de
entre
loin de
pas loin de
près de
tout près de
une commune
un hameau

[A] 🔊

Dialogue   Et vous habitez où?

Student Book p.48

Use the tape to introduce this block. Much of the language will be familiar and the dialogues contain little that is new or that cannot be inferred (*près de, loin de, entre, dans le nord/sud... de*).

After playing the first extract two or three times, ask about Saint-Pol (*petite ville*) and situate it by using the students' general knowledge.

T: Saint-Pol est une ville ou un village? Saint-Pol est dans le Pas-de-Calais, oui ou non? Et le Pas-de-Calais est un...? (département) C'est dans le nord (pointing up) ou dans le sud? (pointing down) Saint-Pol est dans quel département? C'est donc dans le sud? L'ouest? ... Et ce village est près d'une ville? Il est près de quelle ville? (gesture près de) Oui. Arras. Près d'Arras. Répétez « près de ».

You can now introduce *loin de* by contrasting Saint-Pol with where you are and then asking about other places: *Le Canada est près de l'Italie ou loin de l'Italie?*

[B] 🔊

Dialogue   Où est Anvin?

Student Book p.48

This extract allows you to teach *dans le nord/sud/ est/ouest de...* using the map of the *départements* on p.247 of the Student Book, or places in any country. You can also use *entre* in the same way, perhaps also using a sketch.

[C] 🔊

Dialogue   Je suis née dans une commune...

Student Book p.48.

Note that *au nord de* would be more usual here. This is a suitable point to refer to the *Infolangue* on p.48. A small grammar point worth mentioning is that the cardinal points are invariable as adjectives.

[D]

A X kilomètres/mètres/heures/minutes de...

Begin with the location of the college where you are teaching, building up understanding and introducing the phrases gradually. *Kilomètres* and *minutes* will be the easiest for students to understand first.

T: Moi, j'habite une maison en banlieue. Ma maison est à cinq kilomètres du collège. J'habite à cinq kilomètres du collège. J'habite à vingt minutes du collège.

You could put your name and the distances on the board/OHP:

nom	5 km	20 mn

T: Et vous, Malcolm, vous habitez à cinq kilomètres du collège?
M: Non, à deux kilomètres.
T: Bon. Vous habitez à deux kilomètres du collège. Et à combien de minutes?
M: A cinq minutes.

On the board/OHP:

nom	5 km	20 mn
Malcolm	2 km	5 mn

You can build up profiles in this way and then invite students to put questions to each other about what is on the board/OHP.

S1: Deana, elle habite où? / Deana, elle habite près/loin du collège?
S2: (Oui/Non.) Elle habite à dix kilomètres du collège.

You could then move to the distance between towns and use *heures* and *kilomètres*. If you are in a town the names of well known shops can be used to ask how far they are from the centre of town, and thus use *mètres*. You can use the board in the way suggested above. A photocopy of a mileage chart from a road atlas makes a good teaching aid for this.

[E]

Culturoscope – Où vivent les Français?
Cue Cards 4.5 p.121

Student Book p.48

This extract practises numbers and percentages. In order to enable them to practise numbers and convey information, give students the following to do in pairs using the cue cards. The task is for Student A to say the series of numbers from the cue card. Student B has the book open at p.48 and responds by giving the same figure as a percentage and the information associated with it. After A has given five numbers the roles are reversed and B reads the numbers from the cue card. If you wish, you could encourage them to note the information.

A: Trente-cinq.
B: Trente-cinq pour cent des Français habitent dans une ville.
A: (notes 35% – ville)

[F] ((•))
Activity 1

Student Book p.49
This lends itself to note-taking and reporting back and prepares students well for the activity which is

suggested in [I] below. After note-taking and reporting back, students could complete the activity in the book from their notes or from memory.

[G] ((•))
Activity 2

Student Book p.49
When students have listened to the recorded information on the *châteaux* around Paris, ask them to complete the form in their book.

[H]
Activity 3   *Allez-y!*
Activity 4   *Et vous?*

Student Book p.49
Activity 3 prepares students in part for Activity 4, in which they describe the way to their home. This activity can be done in pairs.

[I]
grand(e)/petit(e) ville/village; à... km; au (nord) de...; dans (département); dans le département du/de la...; le département c'est le/la...
Cue Cards 4.6 p.122

Cut the cue cards up and distribute them round the class at random so that each student has one small piece of paper. Students who have question marks on their slips take turns to ask questions out loud in the class. Those who have the information which is being asked for have to provide it. All students note the information for a later feedback session.

S1: Carcassonne, qu'est-ce que c'est?
S2: C'est une ville.
S1: C'est où?
S2: C'est à 92 kilomètres à l'est de Toulouse.
S1: Dans quel département? / C'est quel département?
S2: C'est l'Aude.
S1: C'est où, l'Aude?
S2: C'est dans le sud de la France.

As a follow-up activity, students could report to the rest of the class about who lives where.

Verrières, c'est très petit
Describing a place, Expressing likes and dislikes

Language

adorer
agréable
aimer
animé
assez
beaucoup de
une boulangerie
calme
c'est beau
c'est comment?
une chose
détester
être
les jeunes
joli(e)
humain(e)
au pied de
préférer
de belles propriétés
quand même
un quartier
très
trop de
il y a/il n'y a pas de...

[A]
Adjectives to describe a place: *assez, très*

To introduce this language it may be best to start with the students' own homes. Revise *habiter*, asking where they live etc. and then go into description via *grand* and *petit* introducing *assez* and *très*. You could use the names of towns in France and Britain:

T: Paris est une très grande ville. Leicester est une ville assez grande. J'habite X. C'est une ville assez/très grande.

Go through vocabulary with the students using adjectives where appropriate such as *calme* and *agréable*. Introduce new adjectives such as *industriel*, if needed. You will need to teach questions such as *C'est comment (à X/chez vous)?* Build up descriptions of the places where your students live, noting the language on the board and allowing students to volunteer language: *Comment dit-on 'sports centre' en français?* Encourage students to discuss appropriate descriptions of their town: *Vous êtes d'accord? Je suis/ne suis pas d'accord.*

[B]
Aimer, détester, adorer, il y a..., ne...pas

Present the place where you live, saying whether you like it or not and what there is there. You can set up a contrast with another place. This will enable you to use the negative with *Il y a...*

T: J'habite X. C'est très agréable. J'aime beaucoup X. Il y a un cinéma, trois restaurants. Il y a beaucoup de choses à faire. Je n'aime pas Y. Il n'y a pas de cinéma/ théâtre/restaurant...

Then continue with: *Il n'y a pas beaucoup de choses à faire. C'est trop bruyant...* You could either develop this with your students about the places where they live or you could create contrasting places on the board. In this work you will need the questions: *Qu'est-ce qu'il y a à X? C'est comment? Il/Elle aime X?*

Students could then do a survey in the class whereby they quiz each other on their opinions of the local area. Encourage them to say, *j'aime... parce que...* plus an opinion each time.

[C] ((•))
Dialogue   J'habite à Verrières

Student Book p.50
Play the tape of Danièle Ducreux. It is suitable for note-taking and reporting back. Students hear the tape and give you any information that they can which you note on the board. They hear the tape a few times and then should be able to talk about the village:
Verrières – Loire, petit, lycée, boulangerie.
Danièle – préfère la campagne, les animaux, la nature.

[D] ((•))
Dialogue   Et c'est comment, Montmorency?

Student Book p.50
Do the same process with the tape of Valérie Buil. Linguistic work can be done also before the text itself is looked at.

[E]
Language study

At this point you could look at the *Infolangue* on p.50 and again involve the class by using the language of liking and disliking with their own area or other areas, now that they have more language.

[F] ((•))
Activity 1

Student Book p.51
Do Activity 1 and then seek the opinions of the students about these places if they know them. Students can be invited to say what they can about the places and whether they like them and why or why not. Students can bring their own photos of places they like or do not like and explain their reasons to others in the class in small groups.

[G]
Activity 3   Allez-y!

Student Book p.51
Do the role play suggested in the activity and then invite students to extend the language by inventing other places to talk about using the same pattern of dialogue.

[H] ((•))
Activity 4   Et vous?
Worksheet 4.7 p.123

Student Book p.51
The tape of Corinne talking about Presles could be used in conjunction with Worksheet 4.7 in which the information has been altered.

[I]
Cue Cards 4.8 p.123

Students should now be in a position to talk about where they live in some detail and to talk about other areas also. Using the cue cards, students work in pairs giving and seeking information about the places on their cards which is where they pretend to live. The ticks and crosses on the cards indicate liking and disliking. They can use other language not on the card to talk about where 'they' live of course, and should be encouraged to do so. In order to do this they will need to ask questions: *Où habitez vous? Vous aimez y habiter? Vous aimez X? C'est comment? Qu'est-ce qu'il y a à X?*

Le 17ᵉ arrondissement
Getting to know Paris

Language

une ambiance
anonyme
bourgeois(e)
chic

connu(e)
coupé(e)
encore
un parc
parce que
une partie
populaire
quel(le)
souvent
sympa
vivant(e)
vrai(e)

ordinal numbers

[A]
Ordinal numbers and the arrondissements

You could use the map of Paris on p.53 to introduce and teach the ordinal numbers. This could be introduced in French of course.

T: *Regardez le plan ici.* (pointing) *Il y a des arrondissements. Combien d'arrondissements y a-t-il?*
S: *Vingt.*
T: *Oui. Il y en a vingt. Le premier est au centre. Le vingtième est à l'ouest et le seizième est...?*
S: *A l'est?*
T: *Oui le seizième et à l'est. Où est le dix-huitième?*
S: *Au nord.*
T: *J'habite dans le treizième. Où est ce que j'habite? Dans le nord?*
S: *Dans le sud-ouest de Paris.*

Encourage the students to ask questions of the same type: *Où est le... arrondissement? J'habite dans le... Où est-ce que j'habite? / J'habite où?*

[B] ((•))
Dialogue   J'habite à Paris dans le dixième arrondissement

Student Book p.52
These extracts contain some useful language which can be revised in role play such as, *ça me plaît, j'aime bien.* Play the two extracts to the class a number of times, putting questions in French and asking the class to repeat language. The detail can be put on the board/OHP in note form.

> 10e, agréable, vivant, calme;
>
> 17e, NO, village, sympa, ambiance

Next, interview the students about the areas with no written support other than the words on the board. Encourage them to use the expressions noted above: *ça me plaît, j'aime bien.* The dialogue between Clara and Corinne could also be used for a short transcription practice.

[C] ((•))
Activity 1

Student Book p.52
Students listen to the guide and note which *arrondissement* the monuments are in. This tape could then additionally be used by students to note which part of Paris that is: *centre, nord...*

[D] ((•))
Activities 3 and 4

Student Book pp.52–53
This tape has a lot of language, much of which the students have already come across. After matching the sentences given in the Student Book to the photos in Activity 3 students could go on to the comprehension questions in Activity 4. After doing these activities students could listen to the tape as often as they wish to in groups of two or three and then make a portrait of the *arrondissement.* They should be encouraged not to copy from the tape but to note the key language and to develop their portrait of the area from that language. This could also be a homework activity.

[E]
Points de repère

Student Book p.53
Encourage students to check what they have learned in this unit by testing each other in pairs. They can then record their achievements by filling in the grid provided.

UNITÉ 5 LES COURSES

Language

Qu'est-ce que vous avez comme...?
Qu'est-ce que c'est?
Qu'est-ce que je vous sers?
Vous désirez?
Avec ceci?
désolé
il ne m'en reste plus
Ce sera tout?
c'est tout
d'accord

un ananas
la baguette
le beurre
la brioche
le café
la crème
le croissant
l'éclair
la fraise
la framboise
un gâteau
une glace
le kiwi
la noix
l'orange
le pain
le pain de campagne
une pâtisserie
une pistache
la pomme
la tarte
la vanille

je voudrais...
je vais prendre...
je peux avoir...?
C'est combien?
Ça fait combien?
Je vous dois combien?

à la, à l', au, aux
en

[A]
Asking for things – pâtisseries, fruits, glaces, pain

There is quite a lot of vocabulary in this unit and it needs to be established before the language can be used more extensively with *aux/à la/à l'/au*. Begin by practising *je voudrais/je vais prendre/je peux avoir* with a number of foods. This can be done either with flashcards, magazine pictures or OHP pictures which you point to. Use items with *un/une* or a number: *une/trois baguette(s), tarte(s), croissant(s), brioche(s), éclair(s), pain(s) de campagne, gâteau(x), glace(s); des oranges, fraises, framboises, pommes, kiwis.*

Students ask for these items from you as you show a card or point to the picture. When a student uses *je vais prendre...* the next to buy something must use another of the expressions. A variation on this is to play a cumulative game in which each student asks for the last item(s) and then adds one.

[B]
Asking the price

When students can ask for the items, encourage them to ask for the price as well. Add prices alongside your pictures of food and students can then ask for a combination of items and the price: *Je vous dois combien? C'est combien? Ça fait combien?* Put these phrases on the board/OHP for a while and then remove them, perhaps leaving just: *Je... C'... Ç...*

[C]
Pairwork

Students can then do some pairwork using this vocabulary. Stop the pairwork and remove several of the food pictures explaining that you have not got something: *Désolé(e)/Je n'en ai pas...* Students will then need to use *je vais prendre.../je peux avoir...* rather than *je voudrais...* for their second request. Encourage the use of expressions such as *alors, eh bien*. Pairwork can then be resumed but now Student B can run out of any of the items at will forcing Student A to ask for an alternative.

[D] (())
Dialogue   Bonjour, madame, qu'est-ce que je vous sers?

Student Book p.60
The next learning point is the use of *aux/au/à la/à l'*

with *tarte*, *glace* etc. Play the tape and ask students to pick out any reference to *tarte* and *éclairs* and list the types mentioned. Extend this and list the possible combinations.

> *tarte – aux pommes, fraises, framboises/à l'ananas*
>
> *éclair – au café, chocolat/à la vanille*
>
> *croissant – au chocolat, beurre*
>
> *gâteau – à l'ananas / à la pomme*
>
> *glace – à l'orange, à la pistache, vanille, fraise/au chocolat, café*

Taking the part of the shopkeeper, role play with students, encouraging them to buy a lot of things in the *pâtisserie*, using phrases such as: *Je vous sers. Vous désirez? Je n'en ai pas. Désolé(e)...*

[E] ((•))
Activity 1

Student Book p.61
The tape for Activity 1 gives an example of a dialogue in which the shopkeeper has not got what the customer has asked for. Listen to the tape with the class, asking them to repeat it so that the language is practised again. Note *il ne m'en reste plus*, and explain *en*.

[F]
Cue Cards 5.1 p.124

When you feel they are able to, invite students to use these cue cards which allow the same sort of dialogue to take place. They work with different partners taking turns to be the customer and the shopkeeper. Encourage them to extend the language in any way they can, i.e. how many items do they want? They should do a number of these dialogues with different partners, so give each student a whole set of cue cards.

[G]
Activity 3   Allez-y!

Student Book p.61
This can be done and then students can be encouraged to vary it.

[H] ((•))
Activity 4

Student Book p.61
This can be done and then students encouraged to say what their favourites are in Activity 5. Students can ask each other and to do this, will need to practise the question: *Quel(le) est votre... préféré(e)?*

J'ai acheté du pain, de la viande, des fruits
Saying what you've bought, Shopping for groceries

Language

blanc
une boîte de tomates
les cacahuètes
la chair à saucisses
le chou farci
l'eau (minérale)
dépenser
le fromage
le fruit
le lait
des légumes
un litre d'huile
un morceau de
un œuf
le papier de toilette
le poisson
le raisin
surgelé(e)
rouge
sec
la viande
le vin
le yaourt/yogourt

du, de la, de l', des
perfect tense of *acheter*

[A]
Items of food: du, de la, des

You will find it helpful to make flashcards of the food items for this block. In learning the vocabulary for items of food there are two things to learn – the item and the partitive article *du, de la, de l', des*. These are best acquired if learned as small word groups straight away, i.e. *de la viande*. A practical and active way of teaching these word groups is to have flashcards and to teach: *C'est de la viande, c'est du fromage...* (Put a price on each card for use later.) After repetition and practice, ask students to identify the cards and as they say them correctly so they are handed the card. Other students then have to identify the cards and they get the card in turn if they say the word group correctly, and so on.

[B]
J'ai acheté/dépensé...

Explain that you have been shopping and make statements about the flashcards from [A] above that you take from a shopping bag.

T: J'ai acheté de la viande. J'ai dépensé quarante francs. (40 F is on the card and shown to the class.) *J'ai acheté des cerises et j'ai dépensé douze francs. Donc, j'ai dépensé cinquante-deux francs au total.*

Ensure understanding of the phrases and encourage the class to repeat the phrases. Then put the following questions on the board and give the cards out asking the questions: *Qu'est-ce que vous avez acheté? Combien avez-vous dépensé?*

As soon as possible give the students a task. They note down in any form five things that they have bought, and they put a price to each and total it up. They then find a partner and each asks the questions which they can read from the board at this stage. They exchange the information and then you take feedback and note answers on the board.

T: Alors, Jane, qu'est-ce que Dominic a acheté?
J: Il a acheté des cerises, une salade, des légumes, du pain et une tarte.
T: Combien a-t-il dépensé?
J: (Il a dépensé) 72 francs.
T: Dominic. Vous avez dépensé combien pour la salade?
D: (J'ai dépensé) 4.50 francs.

[C] ((•))
Dialogue   Pardon, madame

Student Book p.62
Ask students to note what the shoppers have bought. They should listen to the conversations a number of times so that they make as exact a note as possible. Some of the words will be new and not in the *Mot à mot* section (*longue conservation, bananes, clémentines*). Ask students to guess at the spelling and meaning. The dialogue can be reconstructed more simply by you with the students. Ask the class to imagine that they are the customers, and you ask them what they have bought. Revise spellings for a moment.

[D] ((•))
Activity 1

Student Book p.63
For this activity play the tape a number of times and then let students do it from memory.

[E] ((•))
Activity 2

Student Book p.63
This activity can be done with no reference to text. Students make notes of the foods mentioned and then they can report back.

[F]
Activity 4   Vous y êtes?

Student Book p.63
These sentences provide more vocabulary practice.

[G]
Activity 5   Et vous?

Student Book p.63
This is suitable for working on in pairs. Students can make up lists which they change in order to work with a second or third partner.

[H]
Culturoscope – La France des fromages

Teach *il est fabriqué...* Then, giving names of cheeses, require students to say where in France they are made: *Le camembert? Il est fabriqué dans le nord/en Normandie.* You could then revise the language of liking/disliking with students as they talk about the various cheeses.

[I]
Cue Cards 5.2 p.125

These cue cards practise items of food and *du, de la, de l', des, avoir acheté/dépensé (je/il/elle/vous* or *tu).*
* Students seek from each other what they have bought and how much they spent. They note this down.
* They circulate and ask any other student:
   1. who his/her partner was and note the name (*Qui était votre partenaire?*)
   2. what he/she bought and spent (*Combien a-t-il/elle dépensé?*)
When this has gone on for sufficient time you can have a report back session in which the students tell you what others bought.

Qu'est-ce que c'est, le cake aux olives?
Asking for an explanation, Understanding quantities for a recipe

Language

les amandes effilées
le bacon
le cake
une cerise
coupé(e)
dénoyauté(e)
l'eau
la farine
l'huile
le jambon
la levure
même
un morceau
les pruneaux
les raisins secs
râpé(e)
le sel
le sucre
le sucre en poudre/vanillé
le verre (moyen)
vert(e)
le vinaigre

la demi-livre (de)
le gramme (de)
le kilo (de)
la livre (de)
un centilitre (de)
un décilitre (de)
un demi-litre (de)
un litre (de)

numbers over 100

Qu'est-ce que c'est le/la...?
C'est quoi...?
Qu'est-ce qu'il y a dans...?
il faut (with recipes)

[A]
Quantities   Photocopy Master 5.3 p.126

Students will need to learn numbers over 100, such as 150, 200, 250 in order to say quantities. Practise just the 100s and 50s for the moment. Identify the measures. Some will be known but *livre, décilitre* and *centilitre* will be new and the two latter need some getting used to. You could use the noughts and crosses game (see Introduction) for a little practice, putting 15 cl, 1 kg, 550 g (= *1 livre*) 1 l (= *1 litre*) in the spaces. Using flashcards, board or OHP link the measures with foods (new *farine* and known *pommes*) and as the students become confident include containers: *un verre, une bouteille, un paquet, un sachet, une boîte.* Encourage students to ask for items with various quantities using a grid of items on an OHP or flashcards. Photocopy Master 5.3 is provided for this purpose. Students will need a lot of practice of these measures in order to feel confident with them, so practise them in:
* shopping with each other
* shopping with you
* dictating amounts to each other: *50 grammes, 1 litre, 15 centilitres...*
* dictating shopping lists to each other: *Il faut – 250 grammes de bacon, un paquet de café...*
This will give variety to the practice. Put an overlay over the OHP and write prices on it.

[B] ((•))
Dialogue   Pour faire le cake, qu'est-ce qu'il faut?

Student Book p.64
Play the tape and ask students to note as much of the recipe as they can. They will need to hear the tape a number of times. Reconstruct the recipe with the students on the board. This will be a good introduction to the following activity in which students ask about the ingredients of recipes. You could photocopy the recipe and then mix up the quantities and ask students to rearrange them, or do the same thing on the OHP.

[C] ((•))
Activity 1

Student Book p.65
This can now be done. It could be done without the aid of the text a second time.

[D] ((•))
Activity 2

Student Book p.65
This activity can be done in pairs or small groups and then gone over together as a reporting back activity.

[E]
Activity 3   Allez-y!

Student Book p.65
This can also be done in pairs. Students can then go on to make up different lists, one giving the item and the partner suggesting the amount.

S1: Du sucre.

S2: Un kilo. (Du) fromage.

[F]
Cue Cards 5.4 p.127

These cue cards provide practice in asking about recipes: *Tu as/vous avez quelle recette?*
Imagining that they are answering questions put by French people, students work in pairs and say what is in the recipes. Distribute the recipes around the class. The task is for students to collect at least four recipes from other students.

S1: Tu as/Vous avez quelle recette?
S2: J'ai le Welsh Rarebit.
S1: C'est quoi, le Welsh Rarebit?
S2: Alors, pour la recette il faut...

Ensure that the students can ask the questions: *Qu'est-ce qu'il y a dans...? Le..., c'est quoi? Qu'est-ce que c'est...?* and that they can say *un peu de/un petit peu de*. They will also need the word *pain grillé/toast*. For preparation ask them to explain to you or each other in French what the following are – a bacon butty, bubble and squeak, trifle, Christmas cake. They have met the language for the main ingredients of these.

Marché ou supermarché?
Saying where you go shopping and why

Language

la boulangerie
au bout de
cher/chère
le choix
faire les courses
l'épicerie
le/la fleuriste
un grand magasin
la librairie
le marchand
la marchande (de légumes)
le marché
meilleur(e)
moins (de)
un petit commerce
pourquoi?
parce que/qu'
plus (de)
pratique
le prix
un produit d'entretien
rapide
je trouve que

aller
faire

[A]
Où est-ce qu'on achète...?

Revise the shops and add new ones by asking where you buy things. It's good to ban the supermarket in this activity. Students should also ask the questions as soon as you have got going. This activity can be done so that *on* is revised with *aller*.

T: Où va-t-on pour (acheter de) la viande?
S: A la boucherie.
T: Et les fruits?
S: On va au marché.
T: Et pour un journal?

[B] ((•))
Dialogue   Où faites-vous vos courses normalement?

Student Book p.66
Play the tape dialogue by dialogue asking the class to identify the shops mentioned, and developing each dialogue with the class. For example, after the first dialogue you can ask someone if they use the supermarket, where it is (revising *il est à... de chez moi*), and why. Their answer can practise the language from the dialogue: *un grand choix*. Repeat the same process for the following dialogues. Discuss reasons with the class, organising the language for them on the board/OHP to give them support at this stage.

Où?	Pourquoi?
Je fais mes courses à la/au...	*plus/moins*
Je vais à la/au...	*trop/plus de/moins de*
J'achète... à la/au...	*prix/qualité*
C'est à... de...	*cher/avantageux/bon*
C'est près de/loin de...	

[C] ((•))
Activity 1

Student Book p.67
This tape is more extensive than the first set of dialogues and can be used to explore more vocabulary and find additional reasons for shopping here or there. Play the tape a number of times and ask the class to identify the shops, then products including new ones, and finally reasons for going to various shops.

[D]
Activity 2   Allez-y!

Student Book p.67
This can be done in pairs. It can then be redone with students using different words in the same type of dialogue.

[E]
Activity 3   Et vous?

Student Book p.67
This is very suitable for pairwork. Students should be encouraged to spend a little time preparing some ideas before beginning.

[F]
Pairwork

The task is for each student to prepare a short narrative about a couple and their shopping. The reason for talking about a couple is to practise the use of *font, vont*. The narrative should have the following framework and can revise the words of frequency such as *parfois, le matin/soir, samedi* etc. Ask students to prepare the narrative and then tell it to another student, who should note it down. Discourage students from writing it all out or writing it in English and then translating it. They should just make notes and talk. An example is given below.

X and Y go ... where?
when? for what? why? where is it?
and they go ...

S/T: X et Y vont au supermarché le soir. Il y a moins de monde et c'est pratique. Ils achètent des choses comme du savon, parce que c'est moins cher. Le supermarché est à six kilomètres de la maison. Le vendredi matin, ils font les courses au marché où ils achètent les légumes. La qualité est bonne/meilleure et les prix sont avantageux. Le marché est au centre-ville. Parfois, ils vont à la boulangerie pour acheter des gâteaux car ceux-ci sont très bons.

[G]
Points de repère

Student Book p.67
Encourage students to check what they have learned in this unit by testing each other in pairs. They can then record their achievements by filling in the grid provided.

UNITÉ 6 TOUTES DIRECTIONS

Language

au coin de
une banque
un camping
un château
descendre
devant
à droite
en face
à gauche
là
monter
la pêche
une pharmacie
une place
un pont
une poste
prendre
une rue
une station de métro
tourner

Il y a un(e)...près d'ici?
Où est...?
vous allez/allez... (je vais)
continuez... (je continue)
vous descendez/montez (je descends/je monte)
vous tournez/tournez... (je tourne)

[A] ((·))
Dialogue   Pardon, madame. Est-ce qu'il y a une pharmacie près d'ici?

Student Book p.70
Revise the places students have already learned using notes or sketches made into a set of flashcards or put on to OHP: *C'est une pharmacie... hôtel, cinéma, banque, piscine, supermarché, boulangerie.* Also, add *château, camping, station de métro* and recycle *bibliothèque, usine, hôpital.*

Play the cassette for students to hear the basics of giving and receiving directions. As each one is heard, write the symbol on the board to reinforce meanings. Rub off or conceal these notes and have students record them in the same way as they hear the recording for the second time.

Use the flashcards of the places to let students hear the question forms they will need: *Il y a une pharmacie près d'ici? Il y a une banque près d'ici?* Then prompt: *Alors, vous posez une question?*
Answer the questions yourself with uncomplicated directions, *oui, c'est sur la gauche/sur la droite/en face*, or with a gesture or quick symbol to reinforce meanings.

[B] ((·))
Activity 1

Student Book p.71
Do the activity with the whole group. Once they have completed the diagram, they could practise simple ways of asking and giving directions in pairs.

[C] ((·))
Activity 2   Photocopy Master 6.1 pp.128-129

Student Book p.71
Use the first seven symbols on the sheet and gradually introduce the following before moving on to a more intensive practice: *allez/continuez tout droit, tournez à droite, tournez à gauche, prenez la première rue à droite/gauche...*
Draw a simple map (or use the one on p.71) and put it on the board, or preferably on OHP. Students suggest where places are and you enter them on a blank outline. Prompt students to ask questions and add to the directions you give them, *descendez la rue/l'avenue* and *c'est sur votre droite/gauche/en face.*

Students are now likely to have a good chance of success of following the directions in the recorded conversations in Activity 2; they will need help with *traverser* and *pont.*

[D]
Practice in asking and giving directions

Use the plan of Montrond-les-Bains on p.71 of the Student Book, or perhaps (first) a simpler map which you draw on the board. A variety of techniques can be used:
* Give increasingly complicated directions which students follow on the map, note and then say where

they end up. This gives them practice in listening before they say the target items themselves.
* Ask students directions to a range of places. Students then give instructions and you can recapitulate them correctly.
* Ask students for directions and then make deliberate mistakes in recaps. Students put you right.
* Get students to ask for and recapitulate directions.

[E]
Cue Cards 6.2 p.130
Activity 4   Allez-y!

Student Book p.71
The cue cards provide information-gap practice for pairs of students. Having done the three pairs of cards, students will have asked for and given directions to nine places and recapitulated what they are told. Note that there are more buildings on the plan than the ones they are to find, so that the third one cannot be located simply by elimination.

Activity 4 should now present no problem to do in class. Alternatively, a written homework could be to write out the dialogues to help consolidate the new vocabulary.

Pour aller à Gare du Nord, s'il vous plaît?
Using the métro in Paris

Language

d'abord
changer
ensuite
jusqu'à
ou
de rien

à, à la, à l', au
descendre (je descends, tu descends, vous descendez)
prendre (je prends, tu prends, vous prenez)
Pour aller...?

[A] ((•))
Dialogue   Pardon, monsieur

Student Book p.72
Before playing the dialogue, read *Culturoscope* on p.73 with the students. Write up the station names which appear in the dialogue, giving each of them a number or letter. Read them out and have the students then read them aloud.

Play the tape. Students write the number or letter of the stations mentioned in the order in which they occur in the dialogue. On a second hearing, stop the tape after the man has given the directions and ask students to recapitulate them as Françoise does.

[B]
Activity 1

Student Book p.72
Give students a few minutes to solve the problems set. You might then ask them to feed back their answers in French: *Pardon, madame/monsieur, pour aller à Concorde, s'il vous plaît?*

[C] ((•))
Activity 2

Student Book p.72
Play the tape and have students feed back their answers in French: *Elle va à Lyon; elle va à la Gare de Lyon; elle prend direction Gallieni...*

[D]
Activity 3   Vous y êtes

Student Book p.73
This activity prepares students for the role play in Activity 4.

[E]
Activity 4   Allez-y!

Student Book p.73
This activity can be extended with a pair practice. Place the métro map on public view, or students look in their book, and ask students to note any two stations of their choice. The first station noted is the starting point, the second the destination. With so many unfamiliar place names, they will need help with pronunciation. Here are two example conversations:

S1: *Je suis à Porte de Clignancourt. Pour aller à Opéra, s'il vous plaît?*
S2: *Eh bien, c'est facile, vous prenez Direction X. C'est direct.*
S1: *Je prends Direction X? Et c'est direct?*
S2: *Oui, c'est cela.*
S1: *Merci, madame/monsieur.*

S1: *Je suis à Châtelet. Pour aller à W?*
S2: *C'est un peu compliqué.* (this needs teaching)
Vous prenez Direction X. Vous changez à Y et vous prenez Direction Z.
S1: *Je prends Direction X. Je change à Y et je prends Direction Z.*
S2: *C'est ça.*
S1: *Merci.*

Au feu rouge
Understanding directions when driving

Language

arriver
en direction de
au feu rouge
en longeant le mur
un panneau
prendre à droite
repartir
retourner à gauche
un stop
à la suite de
suivre
en venant de
vert(e)

C'est loin?
c'est à 500 mètres

[A]
Practice of more complex directions

Student Book p.74
Look again at Photocopy Master 6.1 on p.128. Use it to convey meanings and then to have students repeat and recall the further directions given in this unit: *au premier feu, arriver à un stop, jusqu'à..., en direction de..., au rond-point, au carrefour..., longer le mur du château...* You might make these into a set of flashcards or learning cards.

[B] ((•))
Dialogue   C'est très simple

Student Book p.74
This exchange has the useful phrases, *j'ai tout compris, c'est très clair*. Encourage students to use these in cue card practice and in class too.

[C] ((•))
Activity 1

Student Book p.74
The recording can be used as model dialogues so that students, as well as doing the activities suggested, might try to imitate what is said by the native speakers. Use the cassette to let the students hear the new language. Let them hear the recording two or three times, then ask them to recall any of the language on the cassette.

[D]
Activity 4   Allez-y!

Student Book p.75
This activity can be done as a pair practice (though it is not a communication activity as both students have the information before them), or as a written homework to consolidate the language of this part of the unit.

[E]
Learning cards

Particularly for students having difficulties recalling language, you or they might make sets of learning cards with symbols on one side and the corresponding language on the other. Examples can easily be added to those given on Photocopy Master 6.1: *vous longez le mur du château, en direction de Beaumont, au deuxième carrefour.*

To make these an effective learning resource, students need at least a dozen cards. They look at the symbol, try to recall and say (aloud) the corresponding language and then check by looking at the reverse of the card. If they are right, that card goes to the bottom of the pack; if wrong, they put the card into the middle of the pack, so that it soon comes round again.

Other sets of language can be learned in this way (e.g. all shops by using notes, sketches or English equivalents, and adding new ones to the pack as they occur in the course). The cards can also be used for pairwork. One student can see the picture/symbol/ note and say what it is. The other student checks by looking at the reverse of the card saying, *c'est cela/ non, ce n'est pas cela.*

Le code des panneaux
Recognising road signs

[A]
Quiz

Student Book p.76
Do the quiz activities in class, or set them as part of a homework. You may want to return to this section of Unit 6 when students have learned *on peut, on ne peut pas, on doit, on ne doit pas, il faut, il ne faut pas.* Then they can explain in French those of the signs which give orders rather than information.

[B]
Points de repère

Student Book p.77
Encourage students to check what they have learned
in this unit by testing each other in pairs. They can
then record their achievements by filling in the grid
provided.

UNITÉ 7 À TOUTE VITESSE

Un aller-retour, s'il vous plaît
Buying a ticket, Asking about train times and platforms

Language

un aller-retour
un aller simple
deux aller-retours
deux allers simples
un billet
un chemin de fer
composter
un composteur
un guichet
en première classe
en seconde classe
un train
n'oubliez pas
partir
prochain(e)
une voie
un quai
un retard

le, la, les
Quel? Quelle? Quelles? Quels?

[A]
Preparation for the unit

Practise numbers as they occur in prices, and the 24-hour clock as warm-up activities. Write up 54 F, 100 F, 14 h 05, 8 h 30, 33 F, and have volunteer students read them aloud. Students can then invent prices or times and say them aloud for others to note.

[B] ((·))
Dialogue   Bonjour, madame

Student Book p.80
This is a model tape for students to learn the basic structures and vocabulary needed to buy tickets and to ask for information. Ensure that they understand it thoroughly, then have them imitate Corinne, or the ticket clerk, paying particular attention to the intonations in questions.

[C]
Practice

Buying tickets can be done by providing simple notation and writing up a selection of destinations and ticket types on the board/OHP.

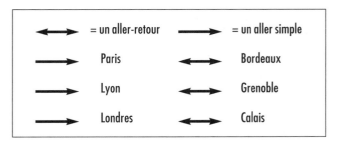

Students choose where they want to go. Play the clerk as in the dialogue with Corinne.

T: Bonjour. Vous désirez?
S: Je voudrais un aller-retour pour Calais, s'il vous plaît.

Then move on to add more details, *1e*, *2e*, and then a price and a platform.

S1: Bonjour, vous désirez?
S2: Je voudrais un aller simple pour Londres, s'il vous plaît.
S1: Oui, en première classe ou en seconde?
S2: Seconde.
S1: Voilà. Cela vous fait 450 francs.
S2: Merci.
S1: C'est sur quel quai?
S2: C'est sur le quai numéro quinze.
S1: Merci, madame.
S2: A votre service, madame.

[D]
Le prochain train pour...
Photocopy Master 7.1 p.131

Use the reduced timetable A from Photocopy Master 7.1 on the OHP to teach the question: *Le prochain train pour Paris est à quelle heure?* Ask the question yourself and students simply say the times they read off the timetable. Then reverse roles. Volunteer students can supply the information.
Give timetable B to a student and write the possible destinations on the board. Students choose a place and ask when the next train leaves for that destination. Either then, or later, add the question and answer about the platform.

[E] ((•))
Activity 1

Student Book p.80
Do this activity as set, then use the recording as model dialogues for students to imitate, predict and recall the information.

[F] ((•))
Activity 2

Student Book p.81
Do this activity and then ask students to cover the French and to recall the English equivalents.

[G]
Activity 3   Vous y êtes?

Student Book p.81
Students can do this activity in class or as a homework. If you do it in class, it can usefully be extended by asking students to write a question of their own in English on a slip of paper and ask other students to find the French.

[H]
Activity 4   Allez-y!

Student Book p.81
Let the students do this individually, then in pairs, where each in turn takes the role of the clerk and the passenger. Check and correct their dialogues as appropriate.

Horaires et prix réduits
Understanding printed information

Language

à l'avance
bénéficier de
blanc(he)
bleu(e)
un calendrier
(vous) choisissez
circuler
les fêtes
en fauteuil roulant
un horaire
janvier
février
mars
avril
mai
juin

juillet
août
septembre
octobre
novembre
décembre
un mois
à partir de
une période
vous ne pouvez pas
un prix
réduit
rouge
sauf
si
un vélo
voyager
un(e) voyageur/euse
une réduction

pour + infinitive

il faut/ il ne faut pas + infinitive

[A]
Teaching the months

Sharing information on birthdays would make a good warm-up activity so that students hear and say at least some of the months. Add le premier (mai).

[B]
Activity 1

Student Book p.82
Let students read the ticket and answer in English. As they suggest answers, say them in French and have some of the students do so also. Much of the language is contained in this unit. 1994 could be shortened to quatre-vingt-dix.

[C]
Activities 2–5

Student Book pp.82–3
Any of these might be set for homework, especially as they all entail reading for information. Alternatively, allow students to work in pairs or small groups nominating a spokesperson to report back the results.

[D]
Timetable

Once the students have found their way round the authentic timetable, use it as a basis for further practice on asking about trains, times and dates.

Je voudrais arriver avant dix heures
Making specific enquiries

Language

une arrivée
avant
changer
côté couloir/fenêtre
demain
un départ
donner
en fin d'après-midi
(non-)fumeurs
proposer
qui
des renseignements
rentrer
réservation obligatoire
un retour
revenir
trop tôt/tard
une voiture

pouvoir (je peux, je ne peux pas, vous pouvez)
devoir (je dois, vous ne devez pas)
vouloir (je veux, je ne veux pas, vous voulez)
je voudrais

[A] ((•))
Dialogue   Je voudrais des renseignements pour aller à Paris, s'il vous plaît

Student Book p.84
For this activity you will need a map of the north of France on the board/OHP. At first hearing, students can pick out the places mentioned and any times they manage to note. Record these as they feed them back to you: *Paris, Hesdin, Arras, 10 h, 6 h 26, 7 h 39, 8 h 08, 8 h 57*. This is also a good opportunity to revise *dans le nord de la France, dans le département du Pas-de-Calais*. Draw the line in on a map and mark the places mentioned and the times at which Françoise will pass through or arrive. On a second hearing, pick out the ways Françoise asks for information: *Je voudrais... alors, je dois changer?*

Ensure that students understand *demain, avant huit heures* and note these expressions. Write *TGV* against the line on the map from Arras to Paris. Students can now try to build a dialogue using the information written on the map with the notes *demain* and *avant 10 h*. It will not be word for word what appears on the

recording, but they have learned enough to communicate in both directions.

Play the recording once more, comparing it with their efforts. They will see that *alors, là, voilà, d'accord, donc* all make the conversation more like real life communication. Encourage them to use some of these in their own exchanges.

[B] ((•))
Activity 1

Student Book p.85
Collect suggestions from students about what belongs in the gaps in the dialogue, one at a time. The completed written dialogue can be used for reading aloud.

[C]
Modal auxiliaries

For practice of *je peux/je ne peux pas*, link them with *possible/impossible* and use the heading POSSIBILITÉS. Students can then make sentences from given notes.

SNCF poss ap 13 h	= Je peux prendre le train à partir de (après) treize heures.
Bus poss	= Je peux prendre le bus.
SNCF imposs av 12 h	= Je ne peux pas prendre le train avant midi.

For *je veux/je ne veux pas*, you might use INTENTIONS as the heading.

bus ✓	= Je veux prendre le bus.
taxi ✗	= Je ne veux pas prendre le taxi.
train ✓	= Je veux prendre le train.
TGV ✓	= Je veux prendre le TGV.
avion ✗	= Je ne veux pas prendre l'avion.

For *devoir*, you might use the heading OBLIGATIONS. Symbols or notes for taxi, bus, TGV, plane, *changer, réserver*, even buying bread etc. (from Unit 5) can prompt. *Je dois prendre un taxi, vous devez changer à Châtelet ...*

The same symbols or notes can be used for *il faut* plus the infinitive. Note that English learners often use the negative, *il ne faut pas* to mean, 'You don't **need** to,' as against '**You mustn't**'. They could usefully be warned of this trap.

[D]

Activity 3   Allez-y!
Cue Cards 7.2 p.131

Student Book p.85
Use the cue cards for further practice and ensure that students understand the notation: *av 12 h = avant midi*, a tick under A/R = *aller-retour*, a cross = *un aller (simple)*. Therefore *av 12 h* can prompt: *Je dois être à Paris avant midi. Je voudrais être à Paris avant midi. Je veux être à Paris avant midi.* Make it clear to them that there is not one right utterance, but at least three. In the same way, *pour quel vol?* is the first reply from the person with card B, but it could equally well be: *Pour quelle destination? Vous allez où? Où allez-vous?*

Show how these cards work by performing one of the tasks with a student. This is a simulated phone conversation. If you do not have access to phones for students to use, asking them to sit back to back for this activity makes it feel more like talking on the phone than having a face to face exchange. The conversation might run as follows.

SA: *Bonjour. Je voudrais des renseignements, s'il vous plaît.*
SB: *Bonjour, madame. Pour quel vol?*
SA: *Pour Lyon, s'il vous plaît. Je dois être à Lyon avant midi, lundi prochain.*
SB: *Oui. Il y a un vol à neuf heures douze.*
SA: *Neuf heures douze?*
SB: *Oui. Arrivée à Lyon, dix heures quinze.*
SA: *Dix heures quinze... Et le prix?*
SB: *Pour un adulte?*
SA: *Oui. Un aller simple.*
SB: *Cela vous fait 950 francs.*
SA: *Et je peux avoir un repas végétarien?*
SB: *Oui, madame.*
SA: *Bien. Merci, madame.*

Encourage students to recapitulate the information they elicit and to note it down.

J'y vais en voiture
Speaking about journeys to work

Language

l'autre bout de
un car
un embouteillage
environ
mettre
une moto

à pied
prendre
rouler
voir
une voiture

je prends, je vais, je pars, j'arrive, je mets (+ time)
ça me prend
use of pronoun *y*

[A] (◦))

Dialogue   Vous mettez combien de temps pour aller...

Student Book p.86
Teach/revise forms of transport: *en voiture, bus, métro, train, car, à pied, vélo, moto.* This is easily done using symbols on the board/OHP.

Ask questions to elicit the simple response *en bus...* Recycle places from earlier in the course: *Comment allez-vous au supermarché? Vous allez comment au bureau? Comment allez-vous/vas-tu au travail?* Show them that *je prends le bus* is an appropriate answer, as well as *(j'y vais) en bus.*

[B]

Times of leaving home, length of journey

Use sketches and notes to help present the new structures. You could start with the third person forms: *Fred part à 7 h, Monique part à 8 h ...*

Next, let students hear first person forms: *Je m'appelle Fred... Le matin, je pars à (vers, entre X h et Y h). Je prends le métro. Je mets dix minutes.*
They are now ready to **answer** questions about their own morning routines.

[C]

Questions

Students now need to practise question forms which they will need for pairwork. This is easily done by putting question marks against the symbols given above: *Vous partez à quelle heure?/Tu pars à quelle heure? Comment allez-vous au travail?/Comment vas-*

tu au travail? C'est loin? Vous mettez combien de temps?/Tu mets combien de temps?

[D] ((•))
Activity 1

Student Book p.87
Use the recording for students to do the task, then use it as a model dialogue.

[E] ((•))
Activity 2

Student Book p.87
Do the activity in class. Extra practice can be provided in *vouloir* and *pouvoir* by having students state their requirements in the first person: *Quel est votre problème? Je suis à Beaumont. Je veux (voudrais) prendre le premier train du matin pour Paris...*

[F]
Activity 3   Vous y êtes?

Student Book p.87
This is best done after intensive practice of the language involved (see [B] above).

[G]
Activity 4   Allez-y!

Student Book p.87
Use this framework for controlled pair practice, before using the cue cards in [I] below.

[H]
Activity 5   Et vous?

Student Book p.87
Students can do this in pairs, noting the information they obtain and feeding it back to the class as a whole: *Alors, Eric va au travail en voiture. Il part à six heures, et il arrive à six heures et demie...*

[I]
Cue Cards 7.3 p.131

For this activity, students will need *vous* and *tu* according to who their partners are. Students with B cards need first to say who they are: *Bonjour, je suis Marie-Eve...*
Students should role play French speakers of their own sex, so care is needed in distributing the cards.

36 15 – Code SNCF
Understanding instructions and using technology

Language

taper	*tapez 3615 SNCF*
composter	*compostez votre billet*
sélectionner	*sélectionnez votre place*
choisir	*choisissez votre train*
prendre	*prenez votre ticket*
introduire	*introduisez votre carte*

[A] ((•))
Activity 1

Student Book p.88
Check that students understand exactly what the instructions they hear on the cassette are, as well as putting them in the right order.

[B]
Activity 2

Student Book p.88
By recapitulating the instructions yourself, you can let students hear first person forms of the verbs: *j'effleure... j'indique...* though it is probably not worth getting students to learn them all.

[C] ((•))
Activity 3

Student Book p.89
Having completed the details, students could do this activity in pairs.

[D]
Points de repère

Student Book p.89
Encourage students to check what they have learned in this unit by testing each other in pairs. They can then record their achievements by filling in the grid provided.

UNITÉ 8 HÔTELS ET CAMPINGS

Vous avez une chambre?
Booking a hotel room, Arriving at a campsite

Language

d'accord
un adulte
avec
un bébé
un camping
une caravane
une chambre
compris
une douche
un emplacement
un (grand) lit
une nuit
par personne
une personne
un petit déjeuner
de la place
réserver
une salle de bains
une semaine
une tente
les WC

[A] ((•))
Dialogue   Bonsoir, madame

Student Book p.92
This dialogue lends itself to building up
comprehension gradually. Give (or ask) the class some
key words using OHP sketches if appropriate:
chambre, lit, douche, salle de bains, compris. Some of
these may be known already to the students. Play the
dialogue without the students looking at the text, and
ask them to give any information they can. This will
mean that they hear the dialogue a number of times.
The basic information to retrieve is: evening/2 people/
double bed/shower, WC, TV costs 250 F/bath, WC,
TV costs 260 F/breakfast is 38 F per head and is
extra/Françoise orders breakfast.

As the information is obtained, sketch it on the
OHP/board as in [C] below (the symbols will be useful
later).

When it is complete, check the French with the class to
see what they can recall, then look at the text in the
Student Book.

[B] ((•))
Dialogue   Bonsoir, monsieur

This dialogue is not given in the Student Book. Use it
in the same way as suggested in [A] above. Students
could infer the meaning of *emplacement*. Use symbols
to depict: *emplacement, caravane, tente, nuit*.

[C] ((•))
Activity 1

Student Book p.93
After students have filled in the grid in the Student
Book as a comprehension exercise, use the booking
dialogues as models. Repeat key phrases and, using
symbols which you can point to, ask students to give
the appropriate language.

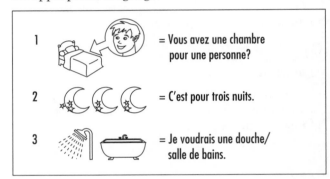

[D] ((•))
Activity 2

Student Book p.93
Students could do this activity in pairs and check it in
class. After doing this you could give students some
reading practice by asking them to read the dialogue
in the correct order to each other while you circulate.

[E]
Activity 3   Vous y êtes?

Student Book p.93
This activity provides consolidation of the phrases
needed to make reservations.

[F]
Whole class practice of reserving a room/site
Photocopy Master 8.1 p.132

Use the Photocopy Master as a basis for class practice.

Students choose their requirements from the given pictures and reserve a room/site from you as receptionist. You then tell them the price from the price list. Other students note the details. They can then report back thus revising the perfect tense in a simple way.

T: Qu'est-ce qu'elle a réservé?
S1: (Elle a réservé) une chambre...
S2: avec un grand lit
S3: et avec une douche
T: Elle a commandé le petit déjeuner?
S: Oui.

You can of course teach *commander* if you wish, then, because they can use two verbs students would be able to say something on the following lines: *Elle a réservé une chambre... et elle a commandé le petit déjeuner.*

[G]
Communicative activity
Cue Cards 8.2 p.133

Students ask each other what is in certain rooms. Their partner provides the information and they fill it in on the card. When the cards are full they check back to see if they got it right. Naturally they do not look at each other's cards when doing the exercise.

S1: Qu'est-ce qu'il y a dans la chambre numéro 36?
S2: Il y a un grand lit, une douche et une télévision.
S1: Et c'est combien la nuit?
S2: 235 francs. Qu'est-ce qu'il y a dans la chambre numéro 44?
S1: Il y a...

[H]
Activity 5   Et vous?

Student Book p.93
Students can phone you to make reservations using the realia. Give them time to work out what they will need to say and try carrying out the phone calls facing away from the student so that there are no gestures to assist understanding.

Nous avons du retard
Apologising, Saying you're late

Language

après
désolé(e)
excusez-moi
je regrette, mais...

à l'appareil
à cause de
la circulation
une demi-heure
dîner
encore
froid(e)
garder
une grève
minuit
en panne
un repas
un retard
avoir du retard
en retard
si
à tout à l'heure
téléphoner
vraiment

j'aurai
j'arriverai
Est-ce qu'on peut...?
Est-ce que je peux...?

[A] ((⋅))
Dialogue   Allô. L'Hôtel des Flandres?

Student Book p.94
Play the tape to the class giving some key language first: *retard, ne pouvons pas, dîner, repas.* Students should be able to work out the general meaning of the conversation with this help. Give them the opportunity to hear the tape three or four times, extending understanding, before looking at the text in the Student Book.

There is quite a lot of vocabulary to use in this block and so students should be given opportunity to go over it carefully before going on to the simple role play suggested in [B] below.

[B]
Role play – phoning to say you are late

Put the following language on the OHP/board as a support for the role play, which will be done with you as receptionist. Ask the students to ring you up and say why they will be late. Encourage the use of the appropriate language for opening and closing phone conversations.

```
... à l'app.
... réservé...
Le train/avion/ferry...          retard.
J'arriverai à...
Désolé(e)/Je m'excuse/Je regrette, mais...
```

These cues can be used to assist students to build up phone calls with you following a set pattern at first. They should be encouraged to use the words of apology as they feel is appropriate. Initially use only the first person singular unless the students feel able to use the *nous* form: *J'ai réservé... Je suis désolé(e)...* Build up to include asking if it would be possible to eat on arrival as is said in the tape extract.

[C] ((•))
Activity 1

Student Book p.94
This activity extends the language to *grève*, *panne* and *circulation*. Note and repeat this language before going on to the extended role play suggested below.

[D]
Extended role play
Choice Framework 8.3 p.134

Using the framework, encourage students to create phone dialogues with you explaining why they will be late using the full range of language available. When you feel that they are confident with this you can ask them to work in pairs. This can also revise earlier material. Students could say where they are: *100 km de l'hôtel/de la ville/du camping.*

[E] ((•))
Activity 2

Student Book p.95
This activity consolidates the learning. When the activity has been done – first by guessing the missing words and then by listening to the tape – ask students to read it to, or with, each other inserting the words as they go.

[F]
Activity 3   Vous y êtes?

Student Book p.95
This activity can be done as pairwork. Students could be encouraged to alter the sentences within the limits of the language of the block.

[G]
Activity 4   Allez-y!

Student Book p.95
These role plays can be varied by using different reasons for lateness, times and names to spell.

[H]
Role play   Est-ce que je peux/qu'on peut...?

After doing Activity 4 you may wish to role play arriving late at a hotel, apologising and asking various things such as whether it is possible to have a meal or if a phone call (to your family in Ireland) is possible. This could then also involve arriving, greeting and apologising, being given your room number and key, checking up about breakfast, making requests about meals and phoning.

La douche ne marche pas
Reporting a problem

Language

une armoire
chaud(e)
le chauffage
une couverture
dès que
il fait bon
ne marche pas
monter
un oreiller
le papier hygiénique
en route
le savon
une savonnette
une serviette (de toilette)
supplémentaire

je pourrais avoir...

[A] ((•))
Dialogue   Monsieur, s'il vous plaît

Student Book p.96
Before listening to the recording, prepare the main vocabulary of the block by giving the nouns from *Mot à mot* on p.96. Then listen to the recording without the students reading the text. Ask the class questions about the content: *Françoise, qu'est-ce qu'elle demande/voudrait? Et où est-il? Et où est l'armoire? Et elle voudrait autre chose aussi – qu'est-ce que c'est?*

[B]
Je pourrais avoir...? Est-ce que je peux avoir...? Il n'y a pas de... ...ne marche pas

Note these phrases with the students and study the examples in the *Infolangue*, on p.96 before doing

Activity 1. Ask the students to note what the phrases are associated with. Do some repetition work of the phrases.

[C] ((•))
Activity 1

Student Book p.96
After doing the activity as suggested in the Student Book use the dialogues for practice by replaying each dialogue completely and then replaying and stopping the tape just before selected parts, asking students to supply the next words.

Tape: – Allô. Réception.
*   – Allô. Ici la...*
S: Chambre 23.
Tape: Il n'y a pas...
S: De serviette...

[D]
Activity 2

Student Book p.97
This can be done by students in pairs and then checked in class.

[E] ((•))
Activity 3

Student Book p.97
This consolidates the language of the block so far.

[F]
Practise complaining/requesting
Photocopy Master 8.4 p.134

Ask the students to give you the items they have already met in the texts that can be reasonably asked for or complained about, adding any others such as *un verre*. List these under the three headings given below as appropriate. Some can be written under two headings of course.

> *...ne marche pas*
>
> *Il n'y a pas...*
>
> *Je pourrais avoir/Est-ce que je peux avoir...?*

Now role play requests and complaints with the class by asking questions: *C'est quelle chambre? Votre nom, s'il vous plaît? C'est Madame... euh? Vous avez regardé dans l'armoire, monsieur? Il n'y en a pas dans l'armoire?* (i.e. for a blanket or pillow)
When you feel that students have acquired the language, or if you feel that they are able to do so straight away, use the Photocopy Master 8.4 which uses illustrations only.

[G]
Activity 4   Allez-y!
Cue Cards 8.5 p.135

Student Book p.97
When you have done this activity, Cue Cards 8.5 can be cut up and used. One set is given to pairs of students who place them face down on a table and then take turns to turn them over making the appropriate request or complaint as they do so. The partner then makes an appropriate reply: *Je suis désolé(e). C'est quelle chambre? Je vous la/le monte. Il y a un/une... dans l'armoire. Oui, tout de suite, madame/ monsieur.*

[H]
Culturoscope   Worksheet 8.6 p.135
Student Book p.97
Further consolidation of the text in the Student Book is provided on Worksheet 8.6.

Châteaux et hôtels indépendants
Understanding information on hôtels

[A]
Reading comprehension

Student Book p.98
This block is mainly for reading comprehension and students should be encouraged to develop dictionary skills. They should be asked to bring dictionaries to the class if they have them. They can of course be shared.

When dealing with the brochure extracts in class (with or without dictionaries) ask the students to give as much information to you as they can about each hotel in turn. They could work at this in pairs first, before whole class discussion and before doing Activity 1.

[B]
Worksheet 8.7 p.136

This worksheet provides extra support for dealing with the brochures.

[C]
Points de repère

Student Book p.99
Encourage students to check what they have learned in this unit by testing each other in pairs. They can then record their achievements by filling in the grid provided.

UNITÉ 9 INTÉRIEURS

J'ai un trois-pièces
Describing your home

Language

une chambre
chez moi
une cour
une cuisine
une dépendance
donner sur
une entrée
entrer
un étage
à l'étage
une marche
une pièce
un rez-de-chaussée
une salle à manger
un salon/séjour
un sous-sol

j'ai une maison
j'habite dans un appartement
il y a deux étages et un sous-sol
au premier étage, il y a trois chambres

je n'ai pas de jardin
il n'y a pas d'ascenseur

[A] ((•))
Dialogue   Dans mon appartement, il y a trois pièces...

Student Book p.106
Play the cassette. Ensure that students see that *salon-salle à manger* is one room only! Do Activity 1 and have students read back their findings.

Using *Chez moi,...* tell them three things about your own home, explaining in French that two are true and one false. They guess the false statement. At this point, or later in the unit, they can do the same and other students guess which of their three statements is false.

[B] ((•))
Activity 2

Student Book p.107
Do the activity, then ask questions in French about the Baudelot house to practise *à tel étage, à côté de...*

[C]
Activity 3   Allez-y!

Student Book p.107
This activity is easily extended by adding *Et vous? (toi?) Et votre (ton) appartement?* as you do each question in class. Alternatively, once the students have answered as though they were Corinne, they could put the same questions, maybe omitting number 3, to others in the class about their own homes.

[D]
Activity 4   Et vous?

Student Book p.107
Students give a short presentation about their home. To show them how they might recycle some of the previously learned language, do two or three yourself. Use the third person to begin with and then describe your real home. Students could note the information in words or symbols: *Monsieur Durand habite un appartement près du centre-ville, à Rouen. Il y a trois chambres, un salon-salle à manger, une cuisine, une salle de bains, et un coin bibliothèque sous les toits. Il travaille dans un bureau, à dix minutes à pied de l'appartement.*
Moi, j'ai une petite maison dans un village, à vingt minutes en voiture de ce collège. J'ai deux chambres, une salle à manger, une salle de bains et un WC séparé. C'est joli comme maison. J'aime bien.

If you think that your class might find such a presentation daunting at first, you could give them cues to follow, and set it as a written homework. But that should be preparation rather than a final piece of work.

[E] ((•))
Activity 5

Student Book p.107
Students will need some help with this as the recordings contain a high proportion of unfamiliar words: *de plein-pied, constituée de, communiquer, pratique.*

The abbreviations should present little problem. The invitation to sell the house might be treated with some humour, in that each feature needs painting in glowing terms. Do some presentation and practice of relevant adjectives and reinforce *il y a...* before students prepare their sales pitch to end the session. They could do this as a paired role-play talking over the phone. This is easily simulated by having them sit back to back.

J'habitais en Seine-et-Marne
Saying where you used to live

Language

auparavant
avant
un couloir
un grenier
un terrain

maintenant:
je suis à Paris
j'ai une maison
il y a cinq pièces
c'est grand
j'habite seul

avant:
j'étais à la campagne
j'avais un appartement
il y avait deux pièces
c'était petit
j'habitais avec mes parents

[A] ((•))
Dialogue   Où étais-tu auparavant?

Student Book p.108
Before playing the tape, use sketches or notes to
introduce/revise some of the language students will
need. These could easily be in the form of a small
advert. Then play the cassette ensuring that students
understand (they may well guess) the meaning of *plus
agréable, plus calme.*

Help them to pick out the words which tell the listener
what used to happen (adverbs, and verbs in the
imperfect).

[B] ((•))
Activity 1

Student Book p.108
Having corrected the errors in the summary, ask
students to give you (from memory – with books
closed) an account of the truth.

[C] ((•))
Activity 2

Student Book p.108
Students can do the straightforward gap-filling
exercise, but will need help with some of the
vocabulary: *moutons, lapins, poules.* Let them hear
the tape to check their answers.

[D]
Activity 4   Allez-y!

Student Book p.109
Once students have established the right order for the
questions and answers, this dialogue is a useful lead-in
to the next activity. Students can read it aloud, playing
the two parts, perhaps in pairs, then try to reconstruct
it from memory.

[E]
Choice Framework 9.1 p.136
Activity 5   Et vous?

Student Book p.109
In preparation for this activity, use the Choice
Framework 9.1. You will need to teach *chien, chat*
and students may well ask you for these words. Use
the same framework to practise the contrast between
past and present. You can do this by choosing two
items from some of the categories.

T: *Avant, j'habitais un château, maintenant, j'ai une
caravane... Avant, j'habitais à Presles, maintenant,
j'habite Rouen.*

Moi, je fais la vaisselle
Saying who does what at home

Language

les carreaux
dépoussiérer
faire la cuisine
faire la lessive
faire les lits
faire le ménage
faire le repassage
faire la vaisselle
faire les vitres
laver
le linge
nettoyer
passer l'aspirateur
Qui fait quoi?
repasser
rester
une tâche ménagère
tous/toutes les deux

c'est moi/toi qui...
elle/lui qui...
nous/vous qui...
ce sont elles/eux qui...

je fais toujours/souvent le ménage
je ne fais jamais la cuisine
je passe l'aspirateur tous les jours
je fais la lessive toutes les semaines
je fais les lits de temps en temps

[A] ((•))
Photocopy Master 9.2 p.137
Dialogue   Je passe l'aspirateur

Student Book p.110
Use Photocopy Master 9.2 to introduce some or all of the household chores vocabulary. These can be used afterwards as an aide-mémoire, to cue either *il/elle fait la vaisselle*, or *je fais la vaisselle*.
Play the dialogues which can then be used as models.

[B] ((•))
Activity 1

Student Book p.111
Play the cassette and do the questions one by one. This allows you to add, *Et vous? (toi?)* so that students can talk about their household chores.

[C] ((•))
Activity 2

Student Book p.111
The focus here is on listening for specific words and phrases. Students will need help with *lourdes, élaborés, une (bonne) partie.*

[D]
Activity 4   Allez-y!

Student Book p.111
Do the first part of the exercise with the class, taking suggestions from individuals. Correct errors and explain that there are alternative ways of expressing the same things.

The second and third interviews can be worked out by the students in pairs. Each plays the role of the interviewer for one interview.

[E]
Activity 5   Et vous?

Student Book p.111
These short presentations are best done in pairs. Revise the question forms before setting the students to work. If you collect all of the questions together and the headings or symbols on the board, students can conduct a survey of the class, or part of it. Even better, they could – if circumstances allow – survey a parallel class.

Styles de vie
Describing homes and lifestyles

Language

beau/belle
bon(ne)
élégant(e)
énorme
grand(e)
gros(se)
joli(e)
vieux/vieille
moderne
petit(e)

[A]
Introduction

Use the illustration to introduce some of the words which students will need in the first activity: *une belle demeure, princière, royale.* For the last two, writing them on the board will help – they **look** like English words, but don't **sound** like them!

[B] ((•))
Activity 1

Student Book p.112
Do the activity with the students. The recording can be further exploited by listening for, and listing on the board:
* all **rooms** mentioned
* the **floors** mentioned
* words which have been learned already (*parfois...*).

You might want to pick up *cinquantaine* and link it with *dizaine*, already seen in the course, and add *douzaine, vingtaine, centaine.*

[C]
Activity 2

Student Book p.112
Do this in class. It is quite difficult as the choices are determined not only by meaning but also by the position of the adjectives.

[D] ((•))
Activity 3

Student Book p.113
Play the cassette and let the students do the gap-filling exercise. Pick out with them, and note, the key words about where people live: *dans les grandes villes, en banlieue, en ville, à la campagne.* Ask questions about their home such as where they used to live, where their

parents lived and whether they have a second home.

[E] ((•))
Activity 4

Student Book p.113
The completed table could easily serve as a stimulus for the students to conduct a questionnaire in class. They need to practise the questions: *Vous avez (Tu as) une voiture? Deux voitures? Le téléphone?*

From the completed survey, students could produce a written report, possibly for homework: *10 sur 12 des étudiants ont une voiture. 90% ont la télévision,...*

[F]
Further practice

As a pairwork activity, students might list their three most important possessions. Before they work in pairs, practise the necessary language with them by making some statements yourself and noting key words on the board:

T: Pour moi, le lave-vaisselle est très important: mon mari ne faisait jamais la vaisselle, avant.
La voiture est essentielle. Je la prends pour aller au travail.
Le téléphone est très utile pour moi: je travaille chez moi, les clients m'appellent.
Nous avons trois télévisions: les enfants en ont une dans leur chambre,

After the pairwork practice, collect some of the reasons students have given to justify their priorities. You might have to correct some error where ambition outstrips present competence. Students could now **write** a short presentation of facts and of their own views, for homework.

[G]
Points de repère

Student Book p.113
Encourage students to check what they have learned in this unit by testing each other in pairs. They can then record their achievements by filling in the grid provided.

UNITÉ 10 LOISIRS

Je fais du théâtre
Talking about your leisure interests

Language

bricoler
la broderie
une carte
chanter
la chorale
la clarinette
les échecs
écouter
en dehors de
l'équitation
une exposition
la gymnastique
jardiner
lire
partir
la pétanque
la planche à voile
une promenade
regarder
le solfège
le théâtre
le tennis
un violon
voir
le volley

faire de (+ pastimes)
jouer à (+ sport)
jouer de (+ instrument)

[A]
Introduction of topic; faire + noun; aimer + noun

As the range of activities which interest people is wide, you will need to introduce this topic gradually. Start by introducing the vocabulary for the various activities and once students are familiar with these, move on to saying what you like to do: *J'aime jardiner, j'aime la télé, j'aime le cinéma...* Next, introduce students to the use of *faire* (*je fais du sport, je fais des promenades...*) before combining both constructions by arranging the vocabulary on the board/OHP under two headings *faire/aimer*. Keep the practice simple at this point. (You may well feel also that you need to introduce *jouer* but if you do you will need to note clearly the different use of *du, de la, de l'*

and *au, à la, à l'*. This can be left until later. See [B] below)

Ask students the question: *Qu'est-ce que vous faites/aimez faire (le week-end)?* and encourage them to say what they do or like doing and provide the language as the need arises. Students too can put the question. As you build up the two lists put the name or initial of the student next to the activity and when the list is complete ask students what other students like to do: *Daniel, que fait Margaret? Qu'est-ce que Margaret aime faire?*

Then ask students to put the question to each other as a whole class activity. In this way you will activate a range of vocabulary and practise students in asking questions in the second and third persons.

[B] ((•))
Dialogue   Et quelles sont les activités...

Student Book p.116
Before playing these dialogues, which should be heard without the book, give the students some key or difficult words – *solfège, en dehors de, lire, broderie*. They may be able to guess the second and last of these. Take the dialogues slowly and use them for comprehension questions. Ask students to tell you about the interests of the various people as each extract is dealt with.

[C]
Infolangue

Student Book p.116
Study the language and the structures. Ask students if they play sports and use the structure: *Je joue au, à la, à l'...*

[D] ((•))
Culturoscope   Activity 1

Student Book p.117
Study the *Culturoscope* by giving percentage figures and asking the class to give the information. Or students could give the figures as well as answer.

T: *Onze pour cent.*
S: *Ils aiment faire des courses (du sport)/Onze pour cent des Français aiment faire les courses (du sport) (le week-end).*

Activity 1 can now be done and the students encouraged to make a note of the activities of the speakers and then report back.

[E]
Class question and answer
Choice Framework 10.1 p.137

In order to give students an opportunity to practise a wide range of the language, use the Choice Framework 10.1. This revises the language of relationships and the possessive adjective and gives a bit more scope for short dialogues. It also contains activities which have not been mentioned in the text but which allow you to follow the interests of students thus extending their vocabulary.

S1: Qu'est-ce que vous aimez faire le week-end?
S2: Je fais de l'équitation, je joue aux cartes et j'aime jardiner.
S1: Avec qui?
S2: Je fais de l'équitation avec ma nièce, et je joue aux cartes avec mes amis. Et je jardine seule. Et vous?

This can of course be done as a whole class activity or by students moving around and working in pairs – or both. There should also be a report back from pairwork and so students should note what their partner says. This will involve the use of *son/sa/ses*.

S3: Claire aime jouer de la guitare et faire des mots croisés. Elle fait des mots croisés avec son mari.

[F]
Cue Cards 10.2 p.138

These cards can be given to pairs of students. They put the pile of cards face down between them and take turns to turn them over. They have to say that they like doing the activity and name a person who they do it with. Alternatively, the sheet of illustrations can be given as it is to students who then point to one picture for their partner to react to.

[G] «⟩)
Activities 2 and 3   Vous y êtes?

Student Book p.117
These activities can be done in pairs before being checked in class.

[H]
Activity 4   Allez-y!

Student Book p.117
Students could work in pairs with one playing the role of interviewer and the other (looking at the Student Book) the interviewee. Students could see how many different ways they know of responding to the questions posed by the interviewer.

[I]
Activity 5   Et vous?

Student Book p.117
When students have done this in pairs they can be encouraged to create personalities for themselves and then to interview each other. Remind them of the categories that they are now able to include as there is a great deal of information – name, relationship, domicile, job, likes and dislikes, activities, etc.

Je ne sais pas nager
Saying what you enjoy doing, what you can and can't do

Language

adorer
avoir horreur de
une bande dessinée
bien
conduire
détester
un dirigeant
une équipe
faire partie de
la lecture
mal
monter à cheval
nager
la pêche
savoir

j'y joue...
j'y vais...
j'en fais...

[A] «⟩)
Dialogue   J'aime bien jardiner

Student Book p.118
This tape can be used to introduce the block. New nouns can be largely understood apart perhaps from dirigeant, which could be given. The verbs nager and savoir are also new and need to be written up. To develop listening skills, play the tape to the class without their reading the text. It can be played in short sections, checking for understanding.
Go over sections more than once, stopping the tape and asking the class to recall what comes next.
Note savoir, which occurs in the text in the je, tu, il and ils forms and practise this as suggested in [B].

[B]
Practising savoir, ne pas savoir

To do this, you could put pin figures plus names on the board/OHP with a symbol or word with ticks or crosses to indicate what the people can and cannot do, (note that *faire de la voile* has been added here).

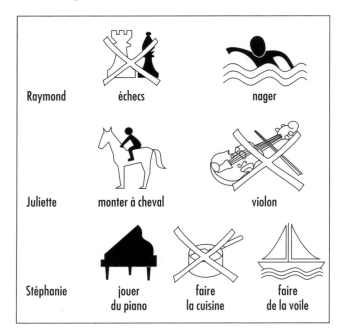

From these cues you can derive statements such as, *Raymond sait nager, (mais) il ne sait pas jouer aux échecs.* Begin by asking, *Raymond, qu'est-ce qu'il sait faire?* and then move on to develop this for the other figures, encouraging students to use the negative. When you feel that the students can manage the construction, ask them what they themselves can do, thus broadening the range of activities. As the sounds of *sait* and *sais* are the same there is an easy transfer.

T: Michael, vous savez faire ça/tout ça?
M: Non. Je sais jouer de la clarinette.
T: Et vous, Susan, vous savez monter à cheval?
S: Oui.

Then make a contrast so that students need to use negatives in their replies.

T: Gail, Vous savez nager et monter à cheval, comme Juliette? (pointing to OHP/board)
G: Je sais nager. (Mais) Je ne sais pas monter à cheval.

When the class has had sufficient practice, present the form of the verb and draw attention to the fact that the verbs *aimer, détester, adorer* are used in a similar way, *J'aime nager.* These can be practised later after Activity 2, see [E] below.

[C]
Infolangue

Student Book p.118
Study the verb structures in the *Infolangue* with the students and deal with any grammar points which may arise. The use of *en* and *y* with expressions of time and the use of *mal* and *bien* are covered below.

[D] ((•))
Activity 1

Student Book p.119
This is a listening comprehension which can be done in class.

[E] ((•))
Activity 2

Student Book p.119
This is a more complex comprehension activity. Students can be encouraged to make notes and then report back as a class activity using the third person. Note *avoir la passion de.* This activity gives a stimulus for practising the use of *adorer, détester, aimer beaucoup* which you could do in the way suggested in [B] above.

[F]
Mal, bien
Choice Framework 10.1 p.137

Students can now talk about what they can do, what they like doing and what they dislike doing. In introducing how well they can do things you may well find that they wish to use *assez*, in which case introduce it. To give a full range of question and answer use the Choice Framework 10.1 to which you may wish to add more of the various activities that your students go in for. Students can be asked to talk about their activities and should be encouraged to say at least three things about each – what they can do, how well they like doing it and how good they are at it. This will use *savoir, aimer, adorer, mal, bien.* They should also say what they do not like doing to activate *ne pas aimer, détester.*

Students can ask each other: *Quelles sont vos activités préférées?* or *Que faites-vous le week-end?* and make notes of two or three conversations and then report back in class.

[G]

Souvent, le week-end, tous les jours, le mercredi

These can be revised if you add another column to the Choice Framework 10.1 or you put the time expressions on the board/OHP. Students can then talk about when they take part in the activities as well as with whom. The time expressions can be cued as follows if you do not want to use the whole word: *souvent* – st; days of week – *l m m j v s d w-e*; *rarement* – r; etc.

You can also revise the time of day at this point including *soir*, *matin* and clock times.

Students can now be encouraged to say: *J'aime beaucoup jouer aux cartes. Je joue assez bien et j'y joue le mercredi soir avec des amis de huit heures à onze heures. Je joue de la guitare le soir et le week-end. Je ne joue pas très bien.*

The use of *y* and *en* can be introduced at this stage. You will need to study the *Infolangue* with the class to facilitate this.

[H]

Activity 3   Vous y êtes?

Student Book p.119
This consolidates the learning and provides a check on what students may be unsure about.

[I]

Activity 4   Allez-y!

Student Book p.119
This is much like a cue card activity. Students can work in pairs before answers are checked in class. Encourage students to make up more 'self portraits' and to interview each other using Choice Framework 10.1 for cues.

[J]

Activity 5   Et vous?

Student Book p.119
This activity could be extended as though it were a first introduction of the student and/or the student's family in the context of a town twinning. The information would then be more extensive than the interests of the student and would include family detail, the place where they live and so on. The activity could either be done as a phone call, acted out in pairs or as homework in the form of a letter.

Je t'invite à déjeuner
Invitations

Language

à vendredi
à tout à l'heure
d'accord
boire un verre
déjeuner
dernier/dernière
devant
c'est dommage
c'est mon tour
comme d'habitude
filer
inviter
libre
malheureusement
regretter
on se retrouve
venir

j'aimerais bien
je veux bien
si tu veux/si vous voulez

[A] «(·)»

Dialogue   Françoise, tu vas au marché jeudi, à Hesdin?

Student Book p.120
Ensure understanding of the tape and use it in small extracts as a model, encouraging the class to repeat and predict when you stop the tape every now and then. Use the tape without the text being read at first and only look at it once the class has done comprehension, listening and repetition work.

[B]

Vous voulez...? Je veux bien. Je regrette... Cue Cards 10.3 p.139

Invite members of the class to do something with you and encourage them to accept or refuse. As you suggest places to go to or things to do, put the item on the board/OHP, as a word or a symbol. You will need to develop these conversations carefully, encouraging rather stock responses at first and beginning with a simple question and answer routine.

T: Norma, vous voulez venir dîner samedi soir?
S: Oui. Je veux bien. Merci beaucoup. / Je regrette. Je ne peux pas.

Places to go and things to do could include:
Culture – *théâtre, cinéma, exposition, concert (pop, musique classique), château à visiter.*
Sport – *tennis, faire du vélo, aller à la piscine/nager, se promener/faire une randonnée.*
General – *café, manger au restaurant, manger chez un/ des ami(s), prendre le café chez quelqu'un, faire des courses avec...*

When you obtain positive replies, suggest days and times, which can again lead to negotiation, and finally add: *On se retrouve où? On se retrouve...à...* This can then lead on to a longer dialogue.
T: Vous voulez venir au cinéma voir Cyrano?
S: Oui. Je veux bien.
T: Vous êtes libre jeudi soir?
S: *Non. (Ce n'est pas possible jeudi. Je ne peux pas jeudi.* Encourage this sort of response so that negotiation has to take place.)
T: Mercredi, alors?
S: Oui. (D'accord. C'est possible.)
T: Très bien. On se retrouve devant le cinéma à dix-neuf heures?
S: Oui. (A dix-neuf heures devant le cinéma.)

Cue Cards 10.3 will help students to develop dialogues along these lines.

[D]
Infolangue
Student Book p.120
When you have completed a number of such dialogues with members of the class you will have a list of items on the OHP or board. Go through them carefully with the whole class while looking at the *Infolangue* section so that they have a clear idea of how to make a request and negotiate.

[E] (())
Activities 1 and 2
Student Book p.121
These activities provide further consolidation of the language before students work more independently. Activity 1 assists with listening while Activity 2 helps with the written form.

[F]
Student pairwork
Ask the students to prepare three or four invitations of different sorts and then ask them to circulate and invite each other out, negotiating about the day, time and the place to meet. Ask them to report back simply, each giving one example of what they will be doing.

S1: *Je vais voir l'exposition Matisse, dimanche, avec Martin. On se retrouve à quatorze heures, devant le musée.*

S2: *Je vais jouer au tennis avec Sylvia. On se retrouve au club à dix heures, mardi matin.*

[G]
Activity 3
Student Book p.121
After doing this activity students can practise giving replies of different types to invitations. In pairs or small groups they can try not to use the reply that the previous speaker used either to accept or refuse an invitation.

[H]
Activity 4   Vous y êtes?
Student Book p.121
This activity can be done by students in pairs.

[I]
Activity 5   Allez-y!
Student Book p.121
This can be done as a whole class activity and the students could be encouraged to write down the replies as well as giving them orally.

Les loisirs des Français
Reading about leisure in France in the 1990s

[A]

This block is mainly reading, but much speaking practice can be derived from it.

[B]
Activities 1 and 2
Student Book p.122
Study the text of the *Préférences de pratiques culturelles* with the class and ask them to identify the words in Activity 1. Go on to Activity 2 which will enable the students to study the language in greater depth. When you have done this, ask students questions relating to the table, from which a considerable amount of language can be developed. Explain and introduce words as necessary.

T: *Vous lisez un quotidien? Lequel? Et vous?*
Qui lit un hebdomadaire? Et un mensuel?
Quels magazines/Quelles revues lisez-vous?
Magnétoscope – Qui possède...? Vous enregistrez des films/documentaires? Vous lisez des romans?
Biographies, livres de voyage...?
Vous sortez pour faire quoi? Pour aller..? Qui fait une collection? Vous collectionnez depuis des ...?; Vous avez combien de...?

[C]
Activities 3 and 4

Student Book pp.122–3
These can be done by students in pairs, and they can
be encouraged to sort out the meaning of the passage
themselves before you look at it as a class. If there are
dictionaries available, encourage their use. Once these
two activities are complete it may be possible,
depending on the level of competence of the class, for
them to give you the meaning of the passage in French
with your help. This involves their using simple
language to convey the meaning.

S: *On écoute beaucoup de musique en France. On
écoute beaucoup plus de musique. On écoute de la
musique à la radio/sur des disques...*

Il y a beaucoup de baladeurs/on achète beaucoup de...
Beaucoup de jeunes/de ménages possèdent...
*Toutes les catégories de la population aiment écouter
la musique.*
*On écoute de la musique pop, de la musique
classique...*
Les jeunes écoutent de la musique chaque jour.

[D]
Points de repère

Student Book p.123
Encourage students to check what they have learned
in this unit by testing each other in pairs. They can
then record their achievements by filling in the grid
provided.

ASSESSMENT UNIT 1-10

The assessments

The assessments cover speaking, listening, reading and writing and are communicative rather than grammatical. The reading and writing assessments could be done by students in their own time if they wish, but the listening and speaking need to be carried out in class. There are no set time limits for any of the assessments as this is left up to your discretion. Students should complete them without reference works. Discuss the assessments with students and encourage them to do them. Prepare them for the assessments by letting them know what they will cover and telling them in advance when the assessment will be. Most of the assessments can be marked by students themselves if you provide the marking scheme. However, the oral assessment does require someone to listen to the exchanges and record marks at that time. Marking schemes are provided after the cue cards.

Oral assessments

To conduct the first oral assessment on exchanging personal details, arrange students in pairs providing each student with a cue card. As assessor you will need a copy of the mark sheet on which you can note the achievement of the task, i.e. that the appropriate items of information have been conveyed. The same arrangement applies to the second assessment in which students arrange to meet. In the third and fourth oral assessments you act as the facilitator taking the part of the shop assistant and the hotel receptionist.
In assessing the students' speech, accept what is understandable to a sympathetic native speaker for the conveying of information and add marks as appropriate for quality.

1. Personal description – seeking and giving information

Working with another student, exchange details about yourselves using the cue cards provided. Make a note of what your partner tells you in any form you wish. There are ten items of information to convey.

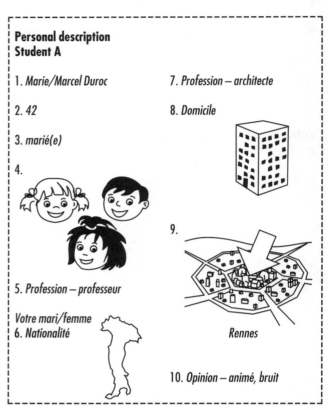

**Personal description
Student A**

1. *Marie/Marcel Duroc*

2. *42*

3. *marié(e)*

4.

5. *Profession – professeur*

Votre mari/femme
6. *Nationalité*

7. *Profession – architecte*

8. *Domicile*

9.

Rennes

10. *Opinion – animé, bruit*

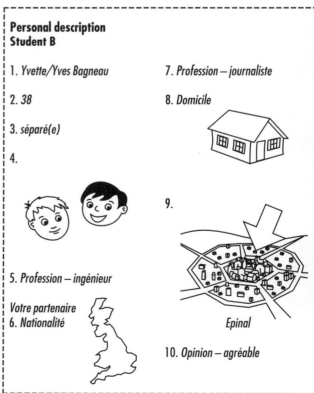

**Personal description
Student B**

1. *Yvette/Yves Bagneau*

2. *38*

3. *séparé(e)*

4.

5. *Profession – ingénieur*

Votre partenaire
6. *Nationalité*

7. *Profession – journaliste*

8. *Domicile*

9.

Epinal

10. *Opinion – agréable*

MARK SCHEMES
1 point for each of the following:
  name
  age
  marital status
  children
  job
  partner's nationality
  partner's job
  home – what? (flat etc.)
  home – where?
  opinion

Items conveyed: ..../10
Quality of French: ..../10
Total: ..../20

2. Invitations

The cue cards provided give cues for suggesting going out and deciding when and where to meet. Do two role plays taking the parts of both A or B in cue card 1 and the alternative role in cue card 2.

Invitations Cue Card 1 Student A	Invitations Cue Card 1 Student B
Suggestion – cinema tonight: 20.00	Can't manage tonight; suggest tomorrow
Agree new day suggested	Ask where to meet
Suggest meet in Café des Saisons at 19 h 30	Accept time and place suggested and repeat them back to make sure

Invitations Cue Card 2 Student A	Invitations Cue Card 2 Student B
Suggestion – meal out tonight	Can't manage tonight; suggest Thursday
Agree new day suggested	Ask where to meet
Suggest meet in Bar Casino at 20 h 30	Accept time and place suggested and repeat them back to make sure

MARK SCHEMES
A, Cue Card 1/2
1 point for each of the following:
  gives invitation   suggests time to meet
  accepts new day   suggests place to meet

Items conveyed: ..../4
Quality of French: ..../6
Total: ..../10

B, Cue Card 1/2
1 point for each of the following:
  accepts idea
  gives alternate day
  accepts time and place
  repeats them back

Items conveyed: ..../4
Quality of French: ..../6
Total: ..../10

3. Shopping

Working with your tutor as the shop assistant, ask for the following items at the baker's and the grocer's. There are ten items in total.

Student: Shopper	Tutor: Shop assistant
Baker's 2 baguettes 3 chocolate croissants one apple tart	**Baker's** You have all the items requested Total cost is 73 francs
Grocer's 1 litre milk 10 eggs 500 gr coffee olive oil 250 gr butter salt 300 gr ham	**Grocer's** You have all the items requested Total cost is 97 francs

MARK SCHEMES
1 point for each of the following:

2 baguettes	500 gr coffee
3 chocolate croissants	olive oil
1 apple tart	250 gr butter
1 litre milk	salt
10 eggs	300 gr ham

Items conveyed: ..../10
Quality of French: ..../10
Total: ..../20

4. Hotel

Working with the tutor as receptionist, book into a hotel using the information on the cue card for your requirements.

Student: Guest at a hotel	Tutor: Receptionist
	Greet the guest
	Ask for how many people
	Ask for how many nights
	You have space
	Offer choice of rooms:
	– 330 F with bath
	– 300 F with shower
	Breakfast is extra – 27 F
	Ask guest to spell his/her name

MARK SCHEMES
1 point for each of the following:

number of people	choose room price
number of nights	ask about breakfast
request for shower/bath	spell name

Items conveyed: .... /6
Quality of French: .... /10
Total: .... /16

Listening assessments

The tapescripts for the listening assessments are printed below and should be pre-recorded with a colleague or a native speaker to be played to the students in class.
Tell the students the format of the first assessment – they will overhear people in the street asking the way to various places. They should mark on their town plan the route taken by the person seeking directions, and label their destination.
Then distribute the town plans, ensuring that everyone knows the starting point, which is marked with an X. Play the tape twice. Students mark in the routes as they

listen. Draw their attention to the *distance* box at the end of the second dialogue. Tell them to fill it in after completing their work on the plans.
For the second assessment, ensure that students know exactly what is expected of them. They may well need some reassurance as they are not expected to note down **everything** they hear, but should focus on the **position** of the gîte, the number of rooms, the facilities and the price. You may like to write those headings on the board.

In giving students their results, make it quite clear that they were not expected to note all the details, and that if they scored twelve, they were doing well. Only if they missed the number of rooms, the number of people the gîte can take, and the price, have they failed to complete the essence of the task.

Tapescript 1

(a)
– Pardon, madame, pour aller à la bibliothèque, s'il vous plaît?
– La bibliothèque? Voyons… alors, vous prenez la première rue à gauche, puis vous continuez jusqu'au rond-point.
– Je prends la première à gauche, et je continue jusqu'au rond-point…
– Et là, vous tournez à droite. Vous longez le parc et après les feux, vous avez la bibliothèque sur votre gauche.
– Je tourne à droite, je longe le parc jusqu'aux feux… et la bibliothèque est sur la gauche.
– C'est ça.
– Merci, madame.

(b)
– Pardon, monsieur, où est la station de métro la plus proche?
– Le métro? Alors, vous descendez la rue là, c'est tout droit, tout droit. Puis vous arrivez aux feux. Là, vous tournez à droite.
– Je vais tout droit et je tourne à droite aux feux.
– C'est cela. Et la station de métro Opéra est tout de suite à gauche.
– Merci, monsieur. C'est loin?
– Non, non, c'est à trois cents mètres.
– Merci, monsieur.
– De rien.

Tapescript 2

Ce gîte-là se trouve à trois kilomètres de la ville. C'est en pleine campagne, alors. Il y a trois chambres à coucher à l'étage, avec lavabo. La salle de bains est à l'étage également, avec WC et douche; puis au rez-de-chaussée, un salon-salle à manger, la cuisine. Tout marche au gaz. Il y a le chauffage central, mais si vous venez au mois de juillet, au mois d'août, ce n'est pas nécessaire. Tout autour, il y a un beau jardin, avec une petite piscine. Alors, comme les chambres sont grandes, il y a la place pour six personnes, ou mettons, deux couples avec trois ou quatre enfants. Les prix pour l'été sont comme ceci: deux mille cinq cents francs par semaine, soit dix mille francs par mois. Si vous voulez réserver, il faut faire vite, hein?

1. Finding the way

Listen to the people asking the way to locations in town. Mark on the map the route they take. All of them start at the station marked X on the map.

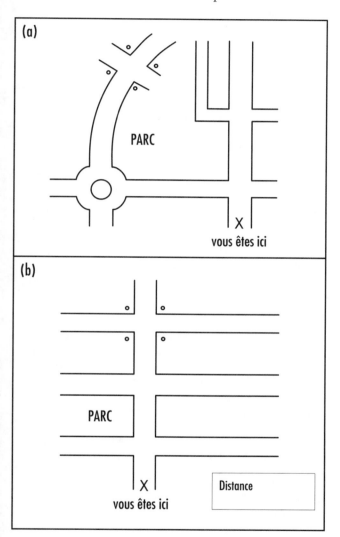

2. House and home

You are interested in booking a gîte in the region of Caussade. You phone to ask for details. This is what you hear about one of the advertised gîtes. Make notes in English on its position, the number of rooms and facilities and the price.

....

....

....

....

....

....

....

....

....

....

....

....

MARK SCHEMES

(a) 1 point for each of the following:
- first left
- at roundabout
- edge of park
- after lights
- library
- on left

(b) 1 point for each of the following:
- straight on
- at lights
- turn right
- on left
- metro station
- distance: 300 metres

Total ..../12

MARK SCHEMES

1 point for each of the following:

3 km from town	lounge-dining room
in the country	on ground floor
three bedrooms	kitchen
on the first floor	all on gas
washbasins	central heating
bathroom	garden
on first floor	swimming pool
toilets	room for six
shower	2500 francs weekly or 10 000 monthly

Total: ..../18

Reading assessments

In preparing students for the first assessment, tell them that what they are going to read is a real letter and therefore may contain words and phrases they have not yet seen. As with the listening assessments, the task is to find the essential information in the text. Make sure that students understand that answers are to be in English.

Before students do the second reading assessment, point out that the article contains some words and phrases which they do not know. Remind them about strategies for making sensible guesses. Ensure that students understand what they have to do – they are aiming to write five short sentences in English putting right the errors in the English summary.

1. Holiday home

A friend who knows little French has had this letter passed on to her. She said she was interested in exchanging houses for her holiday. She wants to know what the letter says, and in particular, where the house is, what is in it and any other facilities offered. Write notes in English to answer her queries.

NB: Do not attempt to translate the letter word for word. Don't worry if there are some parts of it which you don't understand!

```
                              Morteaux
                              le 10 février

Chers amis,
    Ça y est, c'est décidé, nous irons en
Angleterre cet été - si tout va bien! A
cet effet, je cherche à échanger notre
maison   contre   une   maison   (ou   un
appartement)    dans    votre    région.
Connaîtriez-vous  quelqu'un  que  cela
intéresserait? 10 à 15 jours en juillet
ou en août.
    C'est une maison très chouette, genre
ferme ancienne, dans un endroit très
« France profonde », à 10 km de Pontarlier
et à 40 minutes de Besançon.
    Elle est dans un petit village très
sympa qui plaît bien aux touristes et aux
Anglais aussi, car tous les ans il y a
trois ou quatre familles qui occupent des
gîtes. Il y a trois chambres, deux salles
de bains, une cuisine, une salle à manger
avec  une  cheminée,  un  garage,  la
télévision et le téléphone.
    La période peut varier entre le 10
juillet et fin août, mais j'ai une petite
préférence pour la période du 10 au 25
juillet.
    C'est dommage, mais toutes les photos
sont à la Chaux, et non pas ici à
Morteaux, mais si vous connaissez
quelqu'un que cela intéresse, je vous en
enverrai plusieurs.
    J'espère que tout le monde va bien
```

MARK SCHEMES
1 point each for the following:
    looking for house (flat) in the region of the addressee
    10 to 15 days in July or August
    old house (farm)
    10 km from Pontarlier
    40 mins from Besançon
    3 bedrooms
    2 bathrooms
    kitchen
    dining room
    garage
    television
    telephone
    would prefer 10–25 August
Total: ..../13

As with the listening assessments, only if the reader misses the location, the dates possible and preferred and the rooms in the house, have they failed the essential task. However, since other details are easily picked up from the text, most students should score well on this piece.

2. Biopic

Read the French article about Zineb and then look at the English summary of it. The person who did the summary has made five errors. What are they? Answer in English.

> En seize ans, Zineb a vu l'Algérie une petite dizaine de fois. Toujours pour des vacances, un mois ou deux pas plus. Son meilleur souvenir: l'arrivée à Alger en bateau. Quelle émotion! C'était vraiment beau!
>
> Née en France de parents algériens, Zineb ne connaît que le Midi – de Marseille à Nice. Aînée de quatre enfants, Zineb est lycéenne à Bandol, près de Toulon. "Ici, on me considère toujours comme une Arabe. En Algérie, je suis l'immigrée, la Française.
>
> Zineb se définit elle-même comme "une balle de ping-pong sans cesse renvoyée d'un bord à l'autre de la Méditerranée."
>
> Petite, elle rêvait d'être américaine, à cause des films made in USA. Aujourd'hui, l'Algérie, c'est le pays de ses parents. Et la France n'est pas encore le sien. Elle se trouve entre la France, où elle veut vivre et travailler, et l'Algérie où elle retrouve, pendant les vacances, sa culture et sa grande famille.
>
> Ahmed, son père, un maçon de 51 ans, est en France depuis trente ans. Avec une dizaine de familles arabes, ils vivent dans un environnement privilégié, "loin des cités, des banlieues difficiles."
>
> "La France, j'y vis, mais mon pays, c'est l'Algérie." C'est là que vit sa mère, dans un petit village près de Blida. C'est là qu'Ahmed a acheté une maison pour sa retraite, quand les enfants seront indépendants. Zineb a des regrets? Oui, le fait de ne pas parler couramment l'arabe ni de l'écrire. Elle sait écrire son nom et son prénom, c'est tout.

Zineb is sixteen. She has been to Algeria about a dozen times, always in the holidays. She remembers well arriving in Algiers, by boat, and found it a very moving moment.

She was born in Algiers and came to France as a baby. She knows the South of France, from Marseilles to Nice, but that is about all. She goes to school in Bandol, near Toulon. There, she is considered as being thoroughly French, and in Algeria, they think of her as a sort of French immigrant. She says she feels like a ping-pong ball tossed between the two coasts of the Mediterranean.

When she was little, she dreamt of being American, because of the films she saw. Now she wants to find a job in Algeria, because that is where her extended family lives.

Her father is called Ahmed and he is a builder. He lives with a number of other Arab families in some rather troubled suburbs. He thinks of himself as Algerian still, and has recently bought a house in a village near Blida, where his mother still lives.

Zineb wishes she knew more Arabic. She speaks fluently but cannot write much, only her name.

....
....
....
....

MARK SCHEMES
1 point for each error:
  Zineb was not born in Algeria, but in France.
  At school, she is considered Arab, not French.
  She wants a job in France, not in Algeria.
  Ahmed does not live in troubled suburbs: he thinks he is privileged to live away from them.
  Zineb does not speak Arabic.
Total: .... /5

This text and the task cover language seen early in the course, and students should expect to score highly on it (three or four out of five points).

Written assessments

The written assessment has four items. Students can mark these themselves. The degree of accuracy required is a matter for your judgement. Provided the item is almost correct it can be credited. The marks for quality can be used for the level of accuracy. The final item is a translation exercise. Students have done re-translation activities in the units. This assessment is not quite the same, and so students need to be told that the sentences are prompts and not to be translated!

1. Shopping

You want the following shopping. Write out a list so that your French friend can do it for you. Include words such as *un*, *du*, etc. Give figures as figures.

1. strawberry or raspberry tart ....
2. farmhouse loaf ....
3. bananas ....
4. coffee ....
5. biscuits ....
6. lettuce ....
7. small chicken ....
8. 250 gr cheese ....
9. sugar ....
10. 10 eggs ....
11. milk ....
12. 3 yogurts ....
13. pot of jam ....
14. bottle of olive oil ....
15. 500 gr onions ....

MARK SCHEMES
1. *une tarte à la fraise/framboise*
2. *un pain de campagne*
3. *des bananes*
4. *du café*
5. *des biscuits*
6. *une salade*
7. *un petit poulet*
8. *250 gr de fromage*
9. *du sucre*
10. *10 œufs*
11. *du lait*
12. *3 yaourts*
13. *un pot de confiture*
14. *une bouteille d' huile d'olive*
15. *500 gr d'onions*

1 point per *un/une/ du* etc. .... /11
1 point per item .... /15
1 for *tarte, pot, bouteille, petit* .... /4
Quality .... /5
Total .... /35

2. At work

Complete these sentences so that they make sense.

1. *Vous avez besoin d'un billet – allez au ....*

2. *Et n'oubliez pas de .... votre billet avant de prendre le train.*

3. *Est-ce qu'il faut changer? Non, c'est ....*

4. *Je travaille .... Renault, ... secrétaire.*

5. *Je .... quinze minutes pour aller au travail.*

6. *Mon bureau est très proche de chez moi. J'y vais à ....*

7. *Je travaille de huit heures à dix-sept heures, et .... jusqu'à dix-huit, dix-neuf heures.*

1-10 69

8. Mon frère n'a pas de travail, il est ....

9. Et mes parents ne travaillent plus, ils sont à la ....

MARK SCHEMES
1 point per answer
   1. *guichet*
   2. *composter*
   3. *direct*
   4. *chez/comme*
   5. *mets*
   6. *pied*
   7. *parfois*
   8. *chômeur (au chômage)*
   9. *retraite*

Items given: .... /10
Correct spelling: .... /10
Total: .... /20

3. Find the question

Here are answers which were given in interviews where people talked about themselves and their jobs. Write in the question which you think prompted each answer. NB: There are a number of correct solutions.

1. J'ai quinze ans. .... ?

2. Non, je ne travaille pas le mercredi. .... ?

3. J'habite prés de Presles. .... ?

4. Je suis ingénieur. .... ?

5. L'usine est assez loin de chez moi. Je prends la voiture.

.... ?

6. Je termine normalement à dix-sept heures trente ....

.... ?

7. Oui, j'aime beaucoup mon travail. ....

.... ?

8. J'aime bien le tennis, la musique et la lecture. ....

.... ?

MARK SCHEMES

Please note there are many possible questions here. Those which students are most likely to find are given below.
1 point for each of the following:
   1. *Vous avez (Tu as) quel âge? Quel âge avez-vous (as-tu)?*
   2. *Vous travaillez tous les jours de la semaine?*
   3. *Où habitez-vous? (Vous habitez où?)*
   4. *Qu'est-ce que vous faites dans la vie?*
   5. *Comment allez-vous au travail? (Vous allez comment au travail?)*
   6. *Vous terminez à quelle heure?*
   7. *Vous aimez votre travail? (Ça vous plaît, votre travail?)*

8. Qu'est-ce que vous faites pendant votre temps libre? Quels sont vos loisirs?

Questions: .... /8
Accuracy: .... /8
Total: .... /16

(Tutors will need to judge what degree of accuracy gains the point – it does not mean that only 100% accurate answers gain the extra point.)
Students should score at least 10 here.
If they don't, they need more practice in basic questions.

4. Finding the French

Find the French for these situations.

1. You want to attract someone's attention, in the street. It's a man. What do you say? ....

2. A friend asks how you are. You're not feeling at all well. What do you say?

....

3. Someone asks you the way to the supermarket. Tell them that it is 500 metres away, straight along the road. ....

....

4. At the station, you want a single to Rouen. What do you say? ....

....

5. In a café, a friend asks if you would like some olive cake. Tell them that you don't like it. ....

6. Someone asks you if you play badminton. Say that you used to play often when you were young, but that you don't play any more.

....

7. You are in a dance hall. Ask someone if they come here often.

....

8. You are in a hotel. You phone reception to tell them that the shower is not working. What do you say? ....

9. Arriving in the hotel, you want to know where the lifts are. What do you say? ....

10. In a café, you ask for the bill. What do you say? ....

MARK SCHEMES

A point is awarded for each item indicated if it would be understood by a sympathetic native reader.

1. *Pardon, monsieur.* (1)
2. *Ça ne va pas (du tout).* (1)
3. *C'est à cinq cents mètres.* (1) *C'est tout droit (Descendez la rue).* (1)
4. *Un aller (simple) (pour) Rouen, s'il vous plaît.* (1)
5. *(Non) (merci) Je n'aime pas (cela).* (2)
6. *Je jouais* (1) *souvent* (1) *quand j'étais jeune* (1), *mais je ne joue plus* (2) *maintenant.* (1)
7. *Vous venez (Venez-vous)* (1) *souvent là (ici)* (1)?
8. *La douche* (1) *ne marche pas (est en panne).* (1)
9. *Où sont les ascenseurs, s'il vous plaît?* (1)
10. *L'addition, s'il vous plaît.* (1)

Total: ..../19

UNITÉ 11 BON APPÉTIT!

Mon plat préféré, c'est le steack-frites
Talking about your favourite food

Language

à base de
Bon appétit!
en conserve
la (crème) chantilly
dépanner
diminuer
épicé(e)
un four à micro-ondes
les fruits de mer
grâce à
les grillades
un plat
plutôt
rester
un robot ménager
salé(e)
le steack-frites
sucré(e)
tellement

quel, quelle, quels, quelles

[A]
Introducing the topic: naming foods

As this block enables students to say what they like to eat, there is likely to be a wide vocabulary needed. To introduce the topic and revise the foods from Unit 5 give students a time limit to write down as many food words as they can remember. List their items on the OHP/board and begin to comment on them: *Vous aimez les pâtes/la viande/le poisson/les plats sucrés (épicés, salés) n'est-ce pas?* Encourage students to reply using *beaucoup, pas beaucoup*, and teach *tellement. Oui, j'aime beaucoup...*

You can then move on to ask students what they have eaten the day before, or at the weekend, and from this establish further practice in the vocabulary and revise the perfect tense: *J'ai/nous avons mangé, pris, bu...*

[B] ((•))
Dialogue   Quel est votre plat préféré?

Student Book p.126

Introduce the tape and, using it without the text, establish meanings by asking questions. Play the tape again and ask students to make notes about who likes what and then, having checked that they know how to ask the relevant questions, ask them to put questions to each other in pairs about the speakers in order to practise the language: *La femme 1 – Qu'est-ce qu'elle aime manger? Quel est son plat préféré? Anne-Marie? L'homme? La femme 2? La femme 3?* This can be rounded off with a report back session.

[C]
Quel est votre plat préféré?

Ask students about their favourite dishes and widen the questioning to include plural forms (which will require the use of *vos*): *Vous aimez les tartes? Quelles sont vos tartes préférées?* Also introduce *à base de* and *sucré, salé, épicé*. The latter can be used with the negative: *Vous n'aimez pas le curry? Pourquoi? (Parce que) je n'aime pas les plats épicés.*

When you have established the basic language with the students, ask them to put questions to each other about their favourite dishes. This could be done as a mini survey and the results written up for homework.

[D]
Infolangue

Student Book p.126
This would be an appropriate time to look at the *Infolangue* and discuss the forms of *quel*. Afterwards, do a short dictation exercise to reinforce the spelling variations.

[E] ((•))
Activity 1

Student Book p.127
Students can work in pairs for this activity. Give them five minutes to look up as many words as they can to enable them to decide on the answers. Listen to the tape and discuss their answers. Next, give them two or three descriptions of dishes, before they have a go.

[F]
Activity 2   Vous y êtes?

Student Book p.127
Students can be put in small groups to work out the answers to this activity and then report back. Once the translations have been agreed upon, students can work out what the question or answer would be to each of the given sentences.

[G]
Activity 3   Et vous?
Student Book p.127
This activity can also be worked on in pairs or groups before reporting back.

[H]
Activity 4   Quiz
Student Book p.127
When you have done this quiz with the class as suggested in the Student Book, students could develop their own questionnaire to find similar details about their eating habits. The questions could be worked out with the whole class, i.e. *Où est-ce que vous achetez vos produits alimentaires? (supermarché) Vous dépensez à peu près combien par semaine? Avez-vous un congélateur? Aimez-vous manger les produits surgelés? ...*

Students could carry out the survey in the class, or with a parallel class if possible, and then prepare a mini report of their results in French.

[I]
Culturoscope
Student Book p.126
Students can be asked where the various places mentioned are and whether they know anything about the cuisine of the areas. Périgord is well known for truffles, *foie gras*; Lyon for sausage, *saucisson* (Montélimar, famous for *nougat*, is also close by); Alsace for beer and wine; Bourgogne for high-quality wine (*Côte-d'Or, Mâconnais*), snails, *pain d'épice*; Auvergne for cheeses (*cantal*) and *purée de pommes de terre au fromage et à l'ail.*

Un jambon-beurre, s'il vous plaît!
Ordering drinks and snacks

Language

apporter
une boisson
un café crème
un champignon
un cornichon
le croque-monsieur
le jambon
libre
au lieu de
une salade
en salle

service compris
un supplément
à la terrasse
le thon

il n'y a pas de
il n'y a plus de
il n'y a que du/de la/des

[A] ((•))
Dialogue   Bonjour, madame
Student Book p.128
Most of the language of this dialogue will be understandable to the students and so the tape could be played to the class before it is studied in the book to give practice in listening and sorting out meaning. *Thon, jambon, cornichon* and *café crème* are new, and should be given beforehand. Give three or four key questions to the class before they listen to the tape: *Quels sont les différents sandwiches? Que prend Virginie? Qu'est-ce qu'elle veut boire? ...* Play the tape several times, asking the students to listen out for the answers, and then go over it clarifying any points.

When you have done this, use the tape for role play by using the first half ad verbatim, as far as *sandwiches au poulet ou au thon*, and then encourage students to order what they want from the list given by the *serveuse*. Students should do this without using the text, so that they need to hear and recall as they would in a café. Firstly, they can stick to the dialogue as on the tape but once familiar with that, encourage some variation as well.

T: *Qu'est-ce que vous avez comme sandwiches? Vous avez des sandwiches? Je voudrais un sandwich. Qu'est-ce que vous avez? Je vais prendre un sandwich. Qu'est-ce que vous avez?*

[B]
Infolangue
Student Book p.128
Study the *Infolangue*, drawing attention to the *pas de/plus de/que du*, etc. which will be used in the activity suggested in [C] below.

[C]
Using a menu
* Pronunciation and meaning
Look at the menu on p.129 with the class. Some of the words will be familiar but others need to be looked at from the point of view of meaning, *pression, blonde, brune, pamplemousse, comté (fromage)*, and so on, and others for their French pronunciation, e.g. names such as Carlsberg, Pelforth and *décaféiné*. Practise pronunciation by asking the prices of items: *C'est combien la Pelforth brune?* and then encourage

11 73

students to ask for prices, first as a whole class exercise, so that you can assist with pronunciation, and then in pairs for more practice. Note also *un quart* a quarter.

* Ordering and understanding

Tell students that some of the items on the menu are not available today. They must discover which items those are. This will give them plenty of practice in ordering food and asking questions about items on the menu. It will also introduce the *Infolangue* phrases *pas de/plus de* when they have to change their order to something else. Include orders for drinks.

S: *Je voudrais/Avez-vous/Je prends/Je vais prendre un sandwich au jambon, s'il vous plaît.*
T: *Je regrette, monsieur/madame, il n'y a plus de sandwiches au jambon.*
S: *Alors, je vais prendre...*

Students could then do the activity in pairs. One student choosing three or four items only which are still available (it's nearly closing time) and the other trying to determine the items.

[D] ((•))
Activity 1

Student Book p.129
After the activity has been completed, recap by summarising the content of the dialogue with prompt questions: *Il n'y avait pas de...? Qu'est-ce qui s'est passé?* The responses to the first dialogue could include: *Ils ont mangé en salle. Il (l'homme) a commandé un sandwich. Elle voulait une omelette au fromage...*

[E]
Activity 2   Vous y êtes?

Student Book p.129
Some of these sentences can be expressed in more ways than one. Students can work in pairs before going over them as a class activity. Students can also work in pairs on Activity 3.

[F]
Activity 4   Allez-y!
Cue Card 11.1 p.139

Student Book p.129
This activity can be role played between students using the cue cards provided. The student playing the customer can of course vary the responses quite considerably.

[G]
Culturoscope

Student Book p.128
Study the *Culturoscope* with the class, adding information about eating from your own and the class's experience – for example the *trois formules* in restaurants, which usually include a glass of wine and four elements to the meal, the fact that bread is provided and so on. You could also ask a few questions in French: *Où êtes-vous? Il y a un menu à la carte. Vous mangez à quatre heures de l'après-midi? Vous mangez un plat rapide? Vous prenez un café? Vous mangez un sandwich?*

Pour moi, un menu du jour!
Ordering a meal in a restaurant

Language

l'addition
la carte
les chambres d'hôtes
sur commande
un fromage blanc
le menu (du jour)
à la place de
le plateau de fromages
une pomme de terre (au four)
remplacer

je prendrai
on va prendre
pour moi

[A]

The activities in this block relate to different stages of a meal in a restaurant.

[B] ((•))
Activity 1   L'apéritif

Student Book p.130
Define an *apéritif* and ask students to give typical drinks to list on the OHP/board. This will involve pronunciation of such drinks as *un gin-tonic!* Then practise the students in responding to the questions: *Vous désirez/ vous prenez/vous voulez/ je vous sers un apéritif?* Students can respond in a variety of ways: *Je prends... Je prendrai...* (point out that this is the future tense; there is no need at this point to give the whole form) *Je voudrais... Oui. Je veux bien. Je... Un..., s'il vous plaît. Oui, pour moi...*

Use the tape extract to reinforce this. You may have to

teach: *Je ne bois pas d'alcool.*

[C] ((•))
Activity 2   *Le menu*
Activity 3   *Le fromage*

Student Book p.130
Before the students look at the statements 1–6 in their book, ask them to look at the menu, while covering up Activity 2. Then play the tape and ask them to give the meaning as far as they can, using the menu of course to help them. Establish the names of the diners and ask students to note down who orders what. Play back the tape and then do Activity 3 as a group activity. You may like to see how many French cheeses the members of the class can name together.

[D]
Photocopy Master 11.2 p.140

Cut up the words from Photocopy Master 11.2 and place on the OHP, or photocopy and give to small groups of students. Further words can be added to the list from your students' vocabulary. Students can then arrange the words under suitable headings such as, *hors-d'œuvres, viandes, poissons ...*

S: *Je pense que le jambon cru est un hors-d'œuvre.*

Students can then use the class worksheet to give practice in ordering something and in ordering one dish in the place of another. You will need to role play the waiter/waitress. This activity will involve students in using the phrases from the dialogue: *Je prendrai... Je peux avoir... à la place de...?* Students should order the meal as though from the menu, inventing as they wish, and change one dish: *(Est-ce que) je peux prendre/avoir l'escalope de veau à la place de la dinde? ...une quiche aux poivrons à la place de la charcuterie?*

[E] ((•))
Activity 4   *Le dessert*

Student Book p.130
When you have completed this activity you can use the tape as a model for role play with three students ordering desserts from you.

[F]
Activity 5   *Allez-y!*

Student Book p.131
Students can work on this activity in small groups before reporting back and role playing in pairs to the rest of the class. Encourage them to use this as a framework and to include additional phrases if they wish. Any new phrases should be checked with you first.

[G] ((•))
Activity 6

Student Book p.131
This activity can also be done by students in pairs.

S'il vous plaît!
Asking for advice and explanations, Making a complaint

Language

bien cuit
dedans
demander
encore du...
une erreur
à point
recommander
saignant

[A]
Activity 1   *Explanations, recommendations*

Student Book p.132
Go through this activity noting the language which is new and repeating the phrases so that the students can remember them. When you have done this, introduce additional language of things that you may ask for in a restaurant: *du sel, du vinaigre, de la sauce, du poivre, un verre, une fourchette, un couteau, une cuiller/cuillère.*
When these are known, you can put them on the board/OHP in the form of symbols if you wish, or just expect students to rely on their memory in the activity suggested in [B].

[B] ((•))
Photocopy Master 11.3 p.141

This menu will require some clarification to students. This could be in the form of English translations: *la cassolette* is a small dish, *l'éventail de lieu* is an arrangement of hake, *le colin* is also hake, *la bavette* is the undercut of sirloin, *le faux-filet* is sirloin, *l'andouillette* is chitterlings, *Ile Flottante* is custard with floating meringue and caramel. Alternatively, you could write a list of mini-descriptions in French: *Qu'est-ce que c'est la bavette? C'est un steack. La cassolette – c'est un petit plat.* Students are given the mini-descriptions and a cut-up version of the menu and they must match the appropriate items. They can use dictionaries or the Glossary for support and discuss the matter in pairs: *Je pense que... La bavette c'est bon...* A class session can then be held to clarify the meanings. Tell the class that most menus contain the chef's specialities, so it is important to be able to clarify meanings on a menu.

Give students a copy of the menu on Photocopy Master 11.3 or put it on the OHP. Students will now be able to order items, ask for additional things, ask for explanations about the menu or make a complaint: *Vous pouvez m'apporter une cuiller/du sel, s'il vous plaît? Mon poulet est froid. Le colin, qu'est-ce que c'est?*

Activity 2   Allez-y!

Student Book p.132
This activity can be followed by a series of role plays n which students order meals, ask for explanations, request additional things and make complaints. The menus provided in the Student Book and on the Photocopy Master 11.3 can be used for this if further practice is appropriate.

[C]
Points de repère

Student Book p.133
Encourage students to check what they have learned in this unit by testing each other in pairs. They can then record their achievements by filling in the grid provided.

UNITÉ 12 FORME ET SANTÉ

J'ai mal à la tête
Saying what's wrong with you

Language

installez-vous
le bras
un bouton
la dent
le dos
ça vous gêne?
la gorge
la jambe
la main
malade
le menton
le nez
l'oreille
le pied
la tête
tout de suite
le ventre

j'ai mal au, à la, aux...
ça fait mal
ça me fait mal
j'ai froid/chaud/mal au coeur/de la fièvre
je me sens mal/je ne me sens pas bien
je voudrais prendre rendez-vous avec le docteur
Est-ce que je peux voir...?

[A]
Introducing the topic: parts of the body
Photocopy Master 12.1 p.142

Use the Photocopy Master to teach those parts of the body which will be needed in this unit. Identification will involve the question: *Qu'est-ce que c'est?* and the answer *c'est le/la...* and *ce sont les...* As students begin to master this vocabulary, add in, simply for them to **hear**: *Oui, et moi, j'ai mal au/à la/aux...* with groans, grimaces and mimes to match. You can then ask students to say *j'ai mal...* as you indicate various parts of the body on the OHP.

[B] ((•))
Dialogue   Bonjour, entrez

Student Book p.136
Introduce the tape (without the transcription) and on first hearing, ask students simply to indicate (by mime

or in words) the parts of the body mentioned. The rest of the content can be built up by noting it under the following headings.

Problèmes	Symptômes	Durée	Prescription

Point out to students that *prescription* means doctor's orders and not what it looks like. Use *ordres* if you prefer. You will need to help students with *surinfecté*.

[C] ((•))
Activity 1

Student Book p.137
Have the students indicate on a picture of the human body or on themselves where each complaint is located. You can practise this simply by referring to the letter given in the Student Book.

T: f?
S: J'ai mal à la gorge...

[D] ((•))
Activity 2

Student Book p.137
Do the exercise as given. Students' notes, when checked for accuracy, can now be used to practise making appointments. One student, or you, plays the receptionist, and the class supplies language for each of the patients in turn. This will draw attention to useful questions such as: *C'est à quel nom? Ça vous va? Vous avez une préférence?*

[E] ((•))
Activity 3   Vous y êtes?

Student Book p.137
This activity can be prepared and/or extended by use of sketches to prompt. *J'ai mal à la tête...*

Adding a question mark prompts: *Vous avez mal à la tête?* and reference to a third party (*Et votre femme, Eric?*) can cue third person sentences (*Elle a mal à la tête*).

[F] ((•))
Activity 4   Allez-y!
Choice Framework 12.2 p.143

Student Book p.137
This activity is self-correcting. In preparation for it, you may wish to use Choice Framework 12.2.

Quelque chose pour la toux
Obtaining medicines and medical advice

Language

arrêter de
avoir une bronchite
avoir la grippe
avoir une laryngite
avoir un rhume
une boîte
un comprimé
une cuiller à soupe
fumer
un médicament
une pastille
la posologie
un sirop
un suppositoire
tousser
la toux

restez, ne buvez pas, prenez, vous prendrez, il faut prendre, prendre (as instruction)

[A] ((•))
Dialogue   Bonjour, madame

Student Book p.138
Play the recording a number of times, with books closed. Ask questions to establish comprehension: *Quel est le problème de Françoise? Qu'est-ce que la pharmacienne propose? Qu'est-ce que Françoise achète pour la toux? Elle achète autre chose? Elle paie combien?* Students may need help with *C'est tout ce qu'il vous fallait?* and *une tisane.*

[B] ((•))
Activity 1

Student Book p.138
Play the tape and have students do the activity as set. Check answers. With books closed, tell the students what is wrong with you, using the symptoms given in the dialogues; their task is to recall the advice without the text to help them. This can then extend to other problems and advice, as in Choice Framework 12.2.

[C]
Activity 2

Student Book p.139
The activity could well be set for homework, but make sure that you read the text, or at least the answers, aloud, to let students hear a correct pronunciation of them.

[D]
Activity 3   Vous y êtes?

Student Book p.139
These sentences are a straightforward re-cap, but students may have problems with, 'I'd like tablets' which implies preference and not simply a wish and with number 8, which calls for *un mal de ventre* rather than *avoir mal au ventre.*

[E]
Interpreting

Students can carry out an interpreting activity if one of them pretends to be ill and the other translates the complaint to the French-speaking pharmacist. The activity is made more realistic and fun if the interpreter does not know in advance what the others are going to say. Conversations could be set up along the lines of the example given below.

S1: *Would you tell her I've got a sore throat?*
S2: *Mon amie a mal à la gorge.*
S3: *(Elle a mal à la gorge?) depuis quand?*
S2: *How long have you had it?*
S1: *Three days.*
S2: *Depuis trois jours.*
S3: *C'est grave?*
S2: *Is it bad?*
S1: *Well, yes it is.*
S2: *Oui, c'est grave.*
S3: *Alors, voilà des pastilles. Il faut prendre une pastille toutes les deux heures.*
S2: *She wants you to have some pastilles. Take one every two hours.*
S1: *OK.*
S3: *Et puis... peut-être aller chez le médecin.*
S2: *She says maybe go to the doctor.*
S1: *OK.*
S2: *C'est bon. C'est combien?*
S3: *Quinze francs, s'il vous plaît.*
S2: *Fifteen francs.*

[F]
At the chemist   Cue Cards 12.3 p.143

These cue cards provide the stimulus for further transactions at the chemist, but without the interpreting as in [E] above.

Ça va mieux
Saying how you look after yourself

Language

attentif/ve à
en baisse/hausse
les conseils
une couche sociale
éviter
les gens
gras(se)
la moyenne
la nourriture
plus ou moins
la santé
il me semble
suivre
surveiller
à tous les niveaux
de toute façon

je me sens (beaucoup) mieux
ça va mieux

davantage/plus informés
plus de fruits
moins d'alcool
de plus en plus
de plus en plus de...
Quelles sont les maladies les plus courantes?

[A] ((•))
Dialogue   *Est-ce que les gens...*

Student Book p.140
The dialogue is best used simply for comprehension. After eliciting the two or three main pieces of information, you might like to set students a task along the lines of Activity 1, requiring them to find French equivalents in the dialogue for items such as social classes (strata), new illnesses and being careful about what they eat.

[B] ((•))
Activity 1

Student Book p.140
Play the tape and have students do the task as set. You might like to give them the French for the statement which they identify as not being in the dialogue: *Les Français font toujours plus ou moins ce qu'on leur dit (de faire).*

[C] ((•))
Activity 2

Student Book p.140
Play the tape and ask students to note who would have said what. Ensure that they are not expecting to hear the written statements word for word.

[D]
Activity 3   *Vous y êtes?*

Student Book p.141
Do the exercise as set. You can then extend it by having students list all the factors they can which would seem to make for good health, and those which don't. Students could do this for homework, using dictionaries to add one or two to those given in their book.

[E]
Activity 4

Student Book p.141
When students have done the activity, ask them to close their books and see how much of it they can remember. You might want to give them just a few notes or symbols to jog their memories.

[F]
Activity 5

Student Book p.141
The reading exercise could be set for homework. Students might then be asked to talk about the situation in the UK. Since they won't have comparable statistics to hand, they will need to preface their observations with: *J'ai l'impression que... Je pense que...*

Articles from the British press which you come across would be worth keeping, copying and using to prompt oral and written work involving comparisons with France. Students could also use the data to:
* prepare short presentations of their own families
* prepare and then use brief questionnaires in class
* ask a partner about his/her diet and then report the information back to the class.

[G]
Activity 6   *Et vous?*

Student Book p.141
This activity can be done in pairs and threes. Reporting back in the third person ensures that students listen to each other, in order to make notes, and gives the whole class another chance to hear the target language items.

Que faire?
Understanding printed instructions

Language

indications
mode d'emploi
mise en garde
au-delà de
au-dessus
le début
une dose-globule
un état grippal
éventuellement
de façon précoce
laisser
un nourrisson
les sportifs
le traitement
l'usage

[A]
Activity 1

Student Book p.142
Do the activity as set. Students could attempt some or all of the activities in this section for homework. Once the answers have been found and corrected as necessary, you might ask the same questions in French, for oral response. There is scope for using *il faut...* in both questions and answers.

[B]
Activity 2

Student Book p.142
The same techniques can be used as in [A] with this text.

[C]
Points de repère

Student Book p.143
Encourage students to check what they have learned in this unit by testing each other in pairs. They can then record their achievements by filling in the grid provided.

UNITÉ 13 AU TRAVAIL

Le plus beau métier
Explaining what your job is, Making comparisons

Language

actuellement
un chef
les chômeurs
la conception
la direction
à domicile
l'enseignement
une entreprise
la fabrication
la gestion
un métier
je m'organise
un produit
la publicité
responsable de
la restauration
la scène
le secrétariat
la vente

je fais du secrétariat à domicile
je suis/je travaille dans la publicité
je m'occupe de communications professionnelles
plus intéressant que
moins intéressant que
aussi difficile que
le plus beau
le moins cher
le meilleur/le pire
à votre avis/ton avis
je pense que...
je crois que...
pour moi...
à mon avis...

[A]
Preparation

Revise the objectives of Unit 3 on jobs, routines and likes and dislikes. Prompt the relevant question forms with headings: *Travail, distance, commence, finit, opinion.* Student volunteers can put the questions, and others can give answers which reflect the truth or which assume another (French, maybe) identity.

[B] ((•))
Dialogue   *Est-ce que tu travailles?*

Student Book p.150
Play the taped interviews one at a time. With the first one, elicit from the class that the speakers are on familiar terms and use *tu/toi* forms. With each interview, have students fit the essential information under the relevant headings from [A] above and add *métier*.

The first interview contains the useful adverbs *donc, en fait* and *voilà*, in the sense of 'that's right'. Students should note these. You can help by using them whenever possible in classroom talk.

In the fourth interview, the interviewee uses the comparative. Repeat that part of the interview. On OHP/board, quickly sketch a short person and a tall person. Explain the meaning of *plus/moins*. Then move on to discuss jobs which are more or less interesting such as: *chauffeur de taxi* v. *conducteur de métro*.

Allow students to listen to each interview two or three times if necessary. They can then give you a brief summary of each one.

[C]
Activity 1

Student Book p.151
Read the *Culturoscope* aloud for the students and have them read out the sentences after they have had time to prepare them.

[D] ((•))
Activity 2

Student Book p.151
Play the tape and have students add names or initials to the chart given. Then use the completed chart for students to feed back the information gleaned: *Monsieur Parc est directeur de fabrication. Madame Loy est chef du personnel...* They can then check they have got the answers right: *Le Directeur Général, c'est bien X?* Students will need to know actual job titles to do this.

[E] ((•))
Activity 3

Student Book p.151
Before students listen to the tape, define some of the

key phrases for them to help them with meanings: *population active*, *chômeurs*... Then play the tape and have students complete the sentences before they feed back their answers.

[F]
Activity 4   Vous y êtes?

Student Book p.151
This could be set for homework and could easily be extended by asking students to make up another five sentences which re-use language from the unit without simply repeating items from it.

[G]
Activity 5   Et vous?

Student Book p.151
This activity can be set up as group or pairwork. Demonstrate a model with the class first and then students use the questions in pairs or groups. Set a time limit for the activity. Make sure that all students are asking and answering questions. Feedback can be formal or informal, oral or written.

Qu'est-ce que tu vas faire?
Talking about future possibilities

Language

agricole
un apprentissage
l'avenir
un BTS
une carrière
un diplôme
durer
un emploi
les études
une exploitation
une formation
s'installer
une langue
un(e) photographe
performant(e)
un pilote d'essai
poursuivre des études
soit... ou bien...
un stage
à temps plein/à mi-temps
un voyagiste

Tu vas faire quel métier?
tu auras, j'aurai, je prendrai, je travaillerai
je voudrais, j'aimerais bien, j'ai l'intention de

[A]
Future tense

Student Book p.152
Go through the future tense endings given in the *Infolangue*.

[B]
Preparation

Introduce the new professions and trades to the stock of flashcards built up in previous work (*photographe, pilote d'essai, professeur d'anglais, fermier/exploitant*) and revise known vocabulary as you add the new ones in. Explain that the focus here is on future plans. Go over the technical vocabulary, such as *BTS*, before playing the tape.

[C] ((•))
Dialogue   Tes études vont durer combien de temps ici?

Student Book p.152
Focus students' listening during this recording by writing a selection of true/false statements on the board/OHP. Students then have to decide which are true and which are false. They should also correct the false statements. You could then use prompts like these to help students note and feed back the main points: *L'ambition de Christophe, c'est de devenir...; Peggy veut devenir...; Les trois idées d'Amélie sont...*

[D] ((•))
Activity 1

Student Book p.153
In pairs, get students to read through the job adverts before playing the tape.

Students may need help with tenses, sorting out when interviewees are talking about the present, past experience and future intentions. As they hear the interviews for the second time, list the verbs under: *passé, présent, futur*. This is quite an advanced activity and may not be appropriate for all groups.

Their answers to the activity could then be discussed in class: *Quel métier recommandez-vous pour X?*

[E] ((•))
Activity 3   Allez y!

Student Book p.153
This activity can be extended by having students put questions to other members of the class, who make up answers from the language they have been learning.

[F]
Activity 4   Et vous?

Student Book p.153
It would help students to have some practice in the future tense before they do this activity. Write some notes on the board/OHP to serve as prompts:

Maintenant,	je travaille	Dans 10 ans...
	j'ai 55 ans	
	j'habite une grande maison	

Then explain your situation in ten years' time: *Je serai à la retraite. J'aurai 65 ans. J'habiterai à la campagne...* Students could then make up some more prompts for *maintenant* and the class has to put them into the future. This activity could cover a wide range of situations, such as a poor student now and in ten years a managing director. This fun activity will lead them nicely into the activity in their book.

Vive la retraite!
Saying what you used to do, Describing your daily routine

Language

s'ennuyer
se lever
longtemps
s'occuper
un percepteur
se préparer
se promener
se reposer
un restaurateur-hôtelier
se réveiller
le temps
il va y avoir X ans
un voyage

j'étais percepteur
je travaillais dans un bureau
Depuis quand est-ce que...?
je suis à la retraite depuis 1988/trois ans
je travaille ici
je m'occupe, je me repose, je me lève
tu te reposes, t'organises
il/elle se promène, s'ennuie
nous nous reposons, vous vous ennuyez
ils/elles se lèvent, s'organisent

[A]
Preparation
Photocopy Master 13.1 p.144

Use the pictures from the photocopy master to practise talking about students' daily routine with reflexive verbs. Start with the *je* form and then move on to *il/elle*. Once students are familiar with the vocabulary, add times and hold a discussion about the routine of a day in the life of a student. Students can then imagine they are retired and discuss how their routine has changed: *Maintenant, je me lève à dix heures...*

[B] ((•))
Dialogue   M. Soleillant, depuis quand êtes vous en retraite?

Student Book p.154
Play the tape. As students feed back the information, they will have practice in third person reflexives: *Il s'occupe des animaux, il s'occupe des jardins... il se lève assez tard.*

[C] ((•))
Activity 1

Student Book p.155
Ask students to predict the phrases given, then play the tape. On a second hearing, it would be useful to gather together the questions put by Françoise. This is a useful activity in which to highlight spellings. Students will need to refer to the transcript in the Student Book.

[D] ((•))
Activity 2

Student Book p.155
Play the tape, inviting students to take the part of the mother. Ask questions to help them do this: *Ça se passe comment en général, le matin, chez vous?* The activity can be completed quickly in class or at home afterwards.

[E]
Activity 4   Allez-y!

Student Book p.155
After doing the exercise as set, students could work in pairs to create alternative versions. These can also be used in class with students listening, taking notes and then recapping back to the student using the *vous* form.

[F] ((•))
Activity 5   Et vous?
Cue Cards 13.2 p.144

Student Book p.155
Each of these tasks can be done in pairs, where the interviewer's task is to note down what is said (to feed back in the third person if called on) and to prompt with questions when the speaker needs it.

One of the tasks which has not been covered in class could be set as written homework.

This activity can be extended by using the cue cards provided.

Je peux laisser un message?
Phoning for business

Language

Je voudrais parler à (nom), s'il vous plaît
Je pourrais parler à (nom)?
Vous pourriez me passer (nom)?
Ici (nom)
M/Mme (nom), à l'appareil
Je rappellerai plus tard
Il/Elle pourrait me rappeler?
Je peux laisser un message?

C'est moi
Je vous le/la passe
Ne quittez pas
C'est de la part de qui?
Ça ne répond pas
Son poste est occupé
Vous patientez?
Je peux avoir vos coordonnées?
Vous pouvez répéter/épeler, s'il vous plaît?

Vous êtes libre lundi matin?
Non, je suis en réunion
Non, je suis pris(e) toute la journée
Je peux me libérer de 8 h à 10 h/entre 8 h et 10 h
lundi prochain/la semaine prochaine
au mois de juin

[A]
Preparation

On OHP/board write up some of the key phrases/vocab in French. In a second column, write up the English equivalents, but not in the same order. Explain the lesson objectives to the class and ask them to match up the lists in pairs. Give them five to ten

minutes for this. As you go over their answers, practise pronouncing the French with them. Remind them that good, clear pronunciation is very important on the phone as there are no visual clues to support the listener.

[B] ((•))
Activity 1

Student Book p.156
Ask the students if they can recall the language from [A] above. Play the tape again if necessary. The short dialogues can then be used as models for students to imitate and recall.

[C]
Activity 2   Vous y êtes?

Student Book p.156
This can be easily and usefully extended in preparation for the activities which follow. Make sure that each of the five examples is heard and recalled more than once. This is an excellent topic for improvised role play and students could sit back to back to do this. One student is the secretary and the other is the caller. Allow both to improvise using any or all of the language so far covered.

[D]
Activity 4

Student Book p.156
Do the activity as set and then go over the correct solutions: *Elle peut voir Estelle mardi après-midi...*

[E]
Activities 5 and 6   Vous y êtes?

Student Book p.157
Do these as set. In Activity 5 students can read the messages aloud, as well as matching them to the callers.

[F]
Cue Cards 13.3 p.145

When students have done the tasks in this section, they are ready to move on to more open-ended work, using the cue cards provided. Model a dialogue with a student first and ensure that students are aware of the questions they need to ask. A conversation could run along these lines:

A: Allô, bonjour. Ici A.
B: Ah, bonjour. Ça va?
A: Merci. Et vous?
B: Oui, oui. Vous êtes libre lundi?
A: Non, je suis pris(e). J'ai réunion.
B: Et à midi?
A: Non, j'ai rendez-vous.

B: Et mardi? Vous êtes libre?
A: Je regrette, non. Je suis à Strasbourg toute la journée. Mais mercredi, je suis libre. Je suis au bureau entre 9 h et 10 h. J'ai réunion à 10 h.
B: Bien! Moi, je suis au bureau de 9 h à 11 h. Rendez-vous mercredi alors? Neuf heures à mon bureau?
A: D'accord. A mercredi alors. Au revoir.
B: Au revoir.

[G]
Points de repère

Student Book p.157
Encourage students to check what they have learned in this unit by testing each other in pairs. They can then record their achievements by filling in the grid provided.

UNITÉ 14 PLAIRE ET SÉDUIRE

Vous me faites un paquet-cadeau?
Buying presents

Language

apporter
en boîte
un cadeau
chercher
vous connaissez (bien)
coûter
ça dépend
une fleur
le goût
être invité(e)
un paquet-cadeau
soldé(e)
un tableau
en vitrine
vous-mêmes/nous-mêmes

je cherche quelque chose pour une jeune fille
c'est pour faire un cadeau
Qu'est-ce que vous me conseillez?
Je peux regarder?
celui-ci, celui-là, celle-ci, celle-là, ceux-ci, ceux-là, celles-ci, celles-là

[A] ((◦))
Dialogue   Bonjour madame
Worksheet 14.1 p.146

Student Book p.160
To prepare for this recording, revise numbers and prices in the ways which have been most successful for you in past units. Give students a copy of the worksheet to read through before they hear the tape. Allow them to ask (in French) for clarification of any new vocabulary. Play the tape once or twice and check their responses. Then go back over the tape, asking students to pick out key questions and answers: *Je voudrais acheter un cadeau... Qu'est-ce que vous me conseillez? Ils font quel prix?*

[B] ((◦))
Activity 1

Student Book p.160
In addition to the prediction/checking exercise, students can be asked on a second hearing to put the utterances in the right order as they listen to the dialogue again. Focus on the new pronouns and ask students what *celui-ci* might mean. Then use real objects – or empty packets – to teach the language *celui-ci, celui-là...* Offer a choice to students:

T: *Qu'est-ce que vous prenez?*
S: *Des chocolats, s'il vous plaît.*
T: *Ceux-ci ou ceux-là?*
S: *Ceux-là, s'il vous plaît.*

Ask students to suggest a pattern first, then clarify on board/OHP before going on to Activity 3.

[C] ((◦))
Activity 2

Student Book p.161
Ensure that students understand the information in *Culturoscope*. Do the activity. Students might need explanation that *un alcool* is strong liquor and not simply an alcoholic drink.

[D]
Transactions

Practice in transactions can be given by presenting a number of regional specialities for students to buy. This can be given a slight lift if you take in empty packets and explain what was once in them, or a huge lift if you take in full ones! Some examples are given below:
* In a *pâtisserie/confiserie* – *sucre de pomme* (barley sugar) from Normandy; *truffes* (chocolates) from the Alps.
* In a general store – *confit de canard* from the Charente or the Périgueux; *foie gras* from the same regions or Alsace.

You will need to provide prices and it is best to err on the expensive side in the interests of realism!

Je fais du 38
Buying clothes

Language

à la mode
essayer
peut-être
les chaussures
une chemise
un imperméable
une jupe
un maillot de bain
un manteau
un pantalon
un pull/pull-over
une veste
en coton
en cuir
en laine
en soie
blanc(he)
bleu marine
gris(e)
jaune
marron
noir(e)
rose
rouge
vert(e)
clair(e)
foncé(e)
rayé(e)
uni(e)

Vous faites quelle taille?
Vous faites quelle pointure?
je fais du 38/42/46
ça ne (me) va pas
c'est trop grand/petit, long/court
je le prends, je la prends, je les prends
Je peux l'essayer?
Vous l'avez en rouge?

[A] ((•))
Dialogue   Bonjour, madame

Student Book p.162
Teach the vocabulary for clothes and colours using items the class is wearing. Introduce phrases such as: *Ça vous va bien. Le gris, ça ne me va pas. Je préfère le bleu.* Play the first extract of the tape and ask students about what Françoise is buying.

[B] ((•))
Activity 1

Student Book p.163
Play the tape once or twice and invite students to find the information. Use French headings on the board for support:

Vêtement	*Couleur*	*Taille*	*Prix*

[C] ((•))
Activity 2

Student Book p.163
Students read aloud the sentences they are to judge. Play the tape three or four times to do the activities set.

[D]
Activity 3   Vous y êtes?

Student Book p.163
Students may well have problems with pronouns: *c'est, il est, ça me va...* English learners tend to use *ce* when *il/elle* is necessary: *J'aime son manteau: il est bleu.* Using some pictures or the OHP, give a few examples and allow students to spot the pattern. Revise adjective agreements too. Students can now tackle the activity.

[E]
Cue Cards 14.2 p.146

Students can do a role play activity using the cue cards to simulate buying clothes in a shop.

[F]
Activity 4   Et vous?

Student Book p.163
This could be set as a homework activity. It can also be used in class as a basis for pairwork, with one student putting the questions and her/his partner giving the answers prepared at home. The level of difficulty can be raised if questioners work from notes rather than the book: *Manteau – tous les combien? Maillot – tous les combien?*

Un grand brun aux yeux bleus
Describing people

Language

les cheveux bruns/marron
les cheveux grisonnants

les cheveux roux
connaître
court(e)
drôle
frisé(e)
grand(e)
gros(se)
mince
porter
porter des lunettes
raide
sympathique

il est grand/petit/mince/gros
elle est grande/petite/mince/grosse
il/elle fait 1,65m/1,80m
il/elle porte des lunettes
il/elle a les/des yeux marron/bleus/verts/noirs
les/des cheveux bruns/blonds/roux/gris
courts/longs/frisés/raides
il est sympa/drôle/calme/actif/intelligent/patient
elle est sympa/drôle/calme/active/intelligente/
patiente

[A]
Preparation

Collect pictures from magazines, or make sketches, which show those physical characteristics given in the *Mot à mot*. If they include well-known figures such as politicians, singers or athletes, so much the better. Describe the figures, so that students can hear the target items, and understand them without reference to the vocabulary list. This can be done as a quiz with the class guessing the one you are describing.

[B] ((•))
Activity 1

Student Book p.164
Play the tape. Do the first part of the exercise using headings in French. The class should make notes in French. Afterwards, they feed back the details, again in French, with you prompting by asking appropriate questions. Before you finish this activity, write up the question forms. This will prepare students for *Allez-y!* and the remaining activities.

[C] ((•))
Activity 2

Student Book p.164
Once students have completed the activity, they can describe the portrait themselves.

[D]
Activity 3   Vous y êtes?

Student Book p.165
This activity could be set for homework as it is quite

straightforward.

[E]
Activity 5   Et vous?

Student Book p.165
This can be prepared or enlarged on in this way:
* Give verbal portraits of people in the class or of well-known personalities; students identify each.
* Give verbal portraits – students draw.
* Students prepare verbal portraits, read (or say) them aloud; others identify or draw.
* For the self-portrait, they could be given a phone context, arranging to meet someone for the first time. If this is acted out in class, ensure that participants are not face to face. They can describe themselves any way they like or they could describe another person.

Merci mille fois
Saying thank you

Language

merci pour l'excellent repas
une merveilleuse soirée
les fleurs magnifiques
votre carte
merci de nous avoir invités
de m'avoir invité(e)
d'avoir organisé cette journée
merci beaucoup/bien/mille fois!
mille fois merci!

[A]
Preparation

Student Book p.166
Read the text about invitations with the students. Make sure that they do not misread *mondaine* as mundane as it is now used in English!

[B]
Activities 1–3
Cue Cards 14.3. p.147

Student Book p.166
Do the activities as set. As a follow-up, you can use the cue cards to give further pair practice.

[C]
Activity 4

Student Book p.166
This could well be set as a homework, or done in

pairs. Encourage students to keep it simple. You might like to write up an incomplete card on the OHP/board, asking students to fill in the gaps.

> *J'ai été ravi(e) de connaître vos deux enfants; nous avons été très heureux de faire la connaissance de votre ami X et de son épouse...*

[D] ((·))
Points de repère

Student Book p.167
Encourage students to check what they have learned in this unit by testing each other in pairs. They can then record their achievements by filling in the grid provided.

UNITÉ 15 PAR TOUS LES TEMPS

Quel temps fait-il?
Talking about the weather, Understanding weather forecasts

Language

il fait...
beau
chaud
froid
gris
mauvais
il y a...
du brouillard
des nuages
de l'orage
du soleil
du vent
il neige
il pleut

l'automne (m)
l'été (m)
l'hiver (m)
le printemps
une brise
un climat dur
une éclaircie
l'ensemble
fondu(e)
un hiver doux
humide
il manque de vent
la météo
en milieu de journée
un parapluie
la pluie
par rapport à
le temps
un temps lourd

[A]
Introducing the topic

Explain that the topic is about weather and begin teaching the basic vocabulary with the aid of sketches for *il pleut, il fait/il y a du soleil, il y a/fait du vent, il neige, il fait beau/mauvais/froid...* Give plenty of initial repetition using flashcards if possible. Refer to the weather *ce soir* and if you feel that the class can manage it use, *hier il faisait...*

One way of obtaining variety is to attach a type of weather to a town and then ask what the weather is like there. This gives you a range of weather: *à Moscou, il fait froid et il neige; à Cannes, il fait beau.*

[B]
The seasons

Introduce these and use them in the same way as you have used the weather and various towns: *Quel temps fait-il au Canada, en hiver? ...dans le Midi en été? Quand neige-t-il dans les Alpes?* Students can work in pairs or small groups and ask each other what the weather is like anywhere in the world, specifying also the season. Others can reply, inventing suitable conditions.

[C] ((•))
Dialogue   Comment trouvez-vous le climat de Montbrison?

Student Book p.170
Before listening to these dialogues, which include a range of new language, go over the *Infolangue* and *Mot à mot*. Use the tape recordings as a starting point for talking about the climate of the place where you live and of places that students have visited or lived in. This will involve using words such as *d'habitude, souvent, rarement* which you can feed in as needed.

[D]
Weather map   Cue cards 15.1 p.148

Student Book p.171
Study this section which is suitable for reworking language. Questions can be asked such as, *décrivez le climat atlantique*, as this will require students to reformulate the given language: *en hiver le climat est doux./Le climat d'hiver est doux./Il fait doux en hiver.* The cue cards encourage further use of weather vocabulary and seasons.

[E] ((•))
Activity 1

Student Book p.171
Students will need to listen to the tape a number of times in order to make adequate notes. Encourage them to report back after doing the first part of the activity and perhaps listening to the tape again section by section. The answers to the second part of the activity can be worked on in pairs. Students can report back their answers orally.

[F] ((•))
Activity 2

Student Book p.171
The weather forecast uses the future tense which is not really necessary for the students as active language. They may however like to have the system explained. When, or if, you do this, explain also that the future is used relatively infrequently and that a section of Unit 16 will deal with talking about the future.

Play the forecast a number of times to enable students to grasp it fully.

The weather maps can also be used for the present tense description of weather after you have done the activity as set out. Questions can be put by students in pairs to each other about the weather in the various parts of the country.

[G]
Worksheet 15.2 p.149

Use this worksheet to enable students to describe the weather. Students work in pairs. Student A puts weather symbols on his/her map and then tells student B what the weather is like in various parts of the country. The partner who is listening puts weather symbols on his/her map and when the activity is complete the students compare maps. Six maps are given on the worksheet. You may like to run through one first so that the language of north, south, etc. is practised.

[H]
Activity 3	*Vous y êtes?*
Activity 4	*Et vous?*

Student Book p.171
These are suitable for doing in pairs and then reporting back.

Je joue dans un club
Talking about sports, Saying what you used to do

Language

avoir envie de
bronzer
casanier/casanière
le cyclisme
une équipe
essayer de

faire du ski (alpin)
s'intéresser à
même quand/si
la natation
une randonnée pédestre
ressortir
un résultat
un spectateur
une spectatrice
sportif, sportive
ça tourne bien
tous les combien?

imperfect tense

[A] ((•))
Dialogue   Est-ce que tu pratiques un sport?

Student Book p.172
Play the first dialogue to the class two or three times and then ask students to tell you about Fabrice's interests. Clarify meanings fully only after students have first told you as much as they can. There will be some words that are new and RAC may be missed by students also.

Before playing the second part of the tape, ask students to pay attention to the verbs and ask them what they notice. Discuss this and explain that it is the past tense. Then, after playing it two or three times, ask questions, stopping the tape as you go through. For example, after line two you can ask: *Elle pratiquait le football?* and then *Elle le pratiquait tous les combien?*
You can either start discussing the use of the imperfect tense now or when suggested below in [C].

[B]
Revise and introduce new sports

Go over the different types of sports that the class knows and give the French for any others that they suggest, making a list on the OHP/board. You might like to use Choice Framework 10.1 on p.137 for this revision. When you have revised the language of sports and similar activities, students can carry out a class survey asking each other about what they do in their spare time. You will need to include non-sporting activities to reflect the interests of the whole class. Also revise who does various sports and how often. This will prepare the class for the next activities.

[C]
The imperfect tense
Choice Framework 15.3 p.150

Go over the form of the tense and give examples of its use which contrast the present with the past, then discuss the meaning of the tense by asking the students to tell you what they can infer from the examples you give.

T: *J'habitais à X entre 19— et 19—, mais maintenant j'habite à Y.*
Quand j'avais dix-neuf ans, je jouais beaucoup au tennis/j'étais membre d'un club de tennis, maintenant je ne joue plus (pas)/je ne suis pas/plus membre d'un club.
Quand j'étais jeune, j'allais à l'école, maintenant je n'y vais plus.
Quand j'étais plus jeune, je jouais de la guitare; maintenant je joue du piano/préfère jouer du piano.
Il y a cinq ans, j'avais un chien; maintenant je n'en ai pas (plus)/j'ai un chat.
L'année dernière, j'allais souvent à la piscine, mais cette année je préfère faire du vélo.

Encourage the students to make up similar examples, keeping them to the first person singular for the moment. Using the Choice Framework 15.3, practise students in making up statements beginning: *Il y a... ans/Quand j'étais (plus) jeune,... L'année dernière...* They can also use *on* and make statements as below:

S: *Quand j'étais plus jeune, je jouais au tennis dans une équipe. Je jouais deux fois par semaine au club de tennis. Maintenant, je joue rarement – une fois par mois.*
Il y a dix ans je jouais du football avec des amis. On jouait tous les samedis au club municipal. Maintenant je joue au golf.
Quand j'étais plus jeune, je faisais du ski. J'allais en Suisse en hiver. Maintenant je ne le pratique plus, je joue aux cartes.
L'été dernier, j'allais à la pêche au lac Pochin, maintenant j'y vais plus. Il fait mauvais.

When the class has had sufficient practice with your help, students can talk to each other in pairs, inventing the sports and activities they used to do. Suitable questions are: *Est-ce que tu pratiques/vous pratiquez un sport maintenant?...joues/jouez d'un instrument maintenant?... as/avez un passe-temps préféré maintenant?*

[D]
Activity 1   Culturoscope

Student Book p.172
Do this activity and then discuss with the class what sport means to them. Students would need to use such phrases as: *J'aime faire... parce que je.../c'est bon*

pour/on peut/j'aime plus infinitive and *pour moi, c'est...* These could be put on the OHP/board to assist them.

[E] ((·))
Activities 2 and 3

Student Book p.173
Study the questions given in Activity 2 and then play the tape more than once to the class. Ask them to give as much information to you as they can. Then go on to Activity 3.

[F]
Activity 4   Vous y êtes?

Student Book p.173
This can be done by students in pairs.

Sports d'hiver
Choosing a resort from brochures, Discussing facilities

Language

un bowling
un canon à neige
couvert(e), découvert(e)
la détente
l'enneigement
l'entretien
une patinoire
une piste
en plein air
on pourra
tu as raison
une télécabine

si je ne suis pas fatigué, j'irai faire du ski
s'il pleut, on ira...
s'il n'y a pas de neige, on pourra...
si c'est trop cher, je n'y vais pas

[A]
Reading the brochures

Student Book p.174
Students can study the resort brochures in pairs. To do this they may need dictionaries. Ask the students to go through the first brochure and make brief notes so that they can talk about the resort. When they have made notes ask them to close their books and then reconstruct as much information as possible together about Les Menuires on the OHP/board. To do this students will need to re-order and find their own ways of conveying information. Follow this by making a

portrait of Méribel in the same way.

[B]
Infolangue
Choice Framework 15.4 p.151

Student Book p.174
Study the *Infolangue* and then give practice in this
structure by using the Choice Framework 15.4. The
question to ask is: *Qu'est-ce qu'on fait/va faire
demain?* This will permit the following types of reply:

S'il pleut, on pourra jouer aux cartes.
S'il fait du vent, on reste à l'hôtel.
S'il fait beau, on peut/pourra faire une randonnée.
*S'il pleut, on pourra (sortir) manger dans un
restaurant.*

[C] ((•))
Activity 1

Student Book p.174
This is a long tape and it has some quite complex
language in it. As it is also a discussion in detail of
what the resorts offer, you will need to take it slowly
to permit students to make their notes. Play the tape
straight through at least twice to enable students to
tune in to the discussion and note some points. Then
play it through in sections so that they can put ticks in
the grid as appropriate. Check the answers and then
ask students to report back on the opinions of
Frédéric and Aline as you go through the tape another
time.

[D]
Cue Cards 15.5 p.151

These cue cards enable students to practise describing
the facilities and activities available in a holiday
centre. To do the activity, students will need to use the
perfect and the imperfect tenses.

[E]
Activity 2

Student Book p.175
Encourage students to work at this activity in pairs.
They could each take one of the resorts and describe it
to the other and ask questions as well. You could give
the students some assistance with expressions they
will need by revising them first: *...parce que j'aime...
Je n'aime pas... Je déteste... Je préfère... J'adore... Je
trouve que... J'ai décidé de... On va... Nous allons...
Il y a un/une... On pourrait...*

[F]
Points de repère

Student Book p.175
Encourage students to check what they have learned
in this unit by testing each other in pairs. They can
then record their achievements by filling in the grid
provided.

UNITÉ 16 VOYAGES

Je suis parti à la montagne
Saying where you've been on holiday

Language

la chance
la nourriture
nul(le)
sale

perfect tense

[A]
Introduction

In order to revise the perfect tense you could begin with an activity related to holidays the students have taken. Introduce this by saying where you went on holiday in recent years, putting the dates on the OHP/board and using the verbs *passer*, *aller* and *partir*.

> *1993 – Alpes; mars; 8 j; temps*
>
> *1994 – Bretagne; 15 j; été; temps*

T: *En 1994, je suis parti(e) en Bretagne, où j'ai passé quinze jours. J'y suis allé(e) en été. Il a fait très beau pendant la première semaine et puis il a commencé à pleuvoir.*

Students could then be asked about their recent holidays and they could continue to practise in pairs once the language has been sufficiently introduced.

[B] ((•))
Dialogue   Où avez-vous passé vos dernières vacances?

Student Book p.178
The taped dialogues which introduce this section give opportunity to practise the perfect tense fully before analysing its form. Play the first section of the tape and ask what students notice about the tense. Then move on to use it by replaying the first section and putting the bare bones of it on the OHP/board, thus establishing the forms by repetition and questions:

> *Anne Marie*
>
> *Elle est allée au Sénégal*
>
> *Elle a passé 10 jours au Sénégal*
>
> *Elle y est allée avec une de ses filles*

Do the same with the second section of the tape:

> *Hervé*
>
> *Il est parti à la montagne*
>
> *Il a passé 4 ou 5 jours en vacances*

And the third part:

> *Femme*
>
> *Elle est partie à la neige (à Noël)*
>
> *Elle est partie aussi en Guadeloupe*

Ask questions so that students can read the replies: *Hervé a passé huit jours en vacances?* Then rub out the underlined parts and ask questions again. Ask students to note the missing language or get someone to write it in on the OHP/board.

Explain the basics of the system – that some verbs use *être* and some use *avoir* and that the past participle agrees in the former case. Suggest to them that they make their own lists of *être* verbs as they come across them. The most important thing is to give students ample practice.

[C]
Practising the forms

Use students' holidays as a starting point. This will involve *je suis* and *j'ai* of course. Ask where they went on holiday, for how long and who with. Introduce also the weather as the students know that language already. By using *être* in the imperfect (*C'était super...*) you will be giving them a simple way of beginning to understand the difference in the use of the tenses. They should be saying such things as: *Je suis allé(e) à Quiberon. J'ai passé quinze jours en vacances. Je suis parti(e) avec mon amie. Il a fait très beau. C'était très bien/magnifique.*
After some practice of these forms, ask students what they did on holiday. Much of this language is also known: *manger, faire une randonnée, jouer à...., nager ...*

During this stage of the practice it may help students if the forms of the verbs are put on the OHP/board to give support. When they are used, write them in one of two columns *être* or *avoir*.

[D]
Extending the practice
Choice Framework 16.1 p.152

To broaden the range of language, use the Choice Framework 16.1. Students can make up holidays using the framework and add to it with your help. Ensure that you teach the questions which go with each column of the framework so that students can ask each other where they went, etc.

[E]
Infolangue

Student Book p.178
At this stage you may want to discuss the form of the perfect tense and its use with the imperfect in more detail referring to the *Infolangue* section.

[F]
Culturoscope

Student Book p.179
Students can study this alone or better in pairs and then report back and answer your questions on the passage with their books closed. The discussion could be extended to the holiday habits of the British.

[G] ((•))
Activities 1 and 2

Student Book p.179
These recordings give a number of examples of the perfect and imperfect tenses. You will need to play the tape more than once.

[H]
Cue Cards 16.2 p.152

Students work in pairs and can do all three sets of cards. When they have done the cards they can make up holidays for themselves. Ask students to note what their partner says and when the activity is complete, have a report back session in which students describe one of their partner's holidays.

[I] ((•))
Activities 3 and 4

Student Book p.179
When you have done Activity 3 ask the class to study the expressions for a short while and to test each other on them by giving the first word. Then do Activity 4, and follow this by getting students to learn the

positive comments and to test each other. When you have done this, do a role play in which students say how good or bad their holidays were. Use variants of the questions from the taped dialogue, depending on what the student says in reply to the first question. The questions on the tape are: *Tu as passé de bonnes vacances? Qu'est-ce qui s'est passé? Et l'hôtel?* You can add: *Et le temps? Vous avez bien mangé? Qu'est-ce que vous avez fait?*

[J]
Activity 5   Vous y êtes?

Student Book p.179
Students can do this activity in pairs before it is checked in class.

[K]
Activity 6   Et vous?

Student Book p.179
Students should be given a little time to think about an exotic holiday they have had or an invented one and then work in pairs with a number of partners.

Je pense partir dans les Alpes
Talking about holiday plans

Language

un congé
espérer
une famille nombreuse
penser
(tout) de suite

je vais + infinitive
je pense + infinitive
j'espère + infinitive
j'aimerais + infinitive
j'ai l'intention de + infinitive
je pars
je vais partir
je partirai

[A] ((•))
Dialogue   Cette année, qu'est-ce que vous pensez faire?

Student Book p.180
Much of the language is known already. Play the tape in sections and ask students to tell you what they can about the tense use. Also clarify any meanings. Draw attention to the structures (*Je vais/pense partir...*) and ask questions about what the speakers intend to do,

noting the structures on the OHP/board as you use them.

Note how *pour* is used – *Je pars pour... semaines* and also the use of *depuis* with the present tense. Because of the learning load, it is probably best not to introduce the future form at this stage but to deal with that later when the other ways of expressing it have been well established.

[B] ((•))
Activity 1

Student Book p.181
This activity gives more examples of the patterns and could be done at this stage.

[C]
Infolangue

Student Book p.180
Study the *Infolangue*, ask students to close their books and ask what they can recall. Encourage students to use a variety of forms in the activities which follow. Ask them what their plans are now for holidays or visits to friends and relatives. Encourage them to ask each other: *Que pensez-vous faire pour vos vacances? Où allez-vous en vacances? Vous avez des projets de visites? Quand est-ce que vous partez? Avec qui? Pour combien de temps? Qu'est-ce que vous allez faire?*

Extend the practice by using the Choice Framework 16.1 on p.152. The column for the weather does not fit this exercise and needs to be covered over. You could, however, add symbols for types of travel and include the questions: *Vous allez voyager comment? Vous prenez le bateau/le train/la voiture/ l'aéroglisseur? Vous partez en vélo, moto, voiture? Vous passez par le tunnel?*

[D]
Culturoscope

Student Book p.181
Discuss this with students and compare their holiday entitlements to the French pattern.

[E]
Activity 2   Vous y êtes?

Student Book p.181
Students can do this activity in pairs before reporting back as a class exercise. For further practice, students could work in groups of four. Each student chooses a specific requirement for a holiday, i.e. A likes the seaside, B likes hot weather, C likes sport, etc. They then have to discuss suitable locations and agree upon a holiday destination.

[F]
Activity 3   Allez-y!

Student Book p.181
Ask students to work out what they could say using the cues in the Student Book. After you have practised this role play it can be varied.

Ma voiture ne démarre pas
Coping with a car breakdown

Language

la batterie
le capot
le clignotant
le coffre
une crevaison
l'essuie-glace
le frein
le klaxon
le moteur
le pare-brise
les phares
le rétroviseur
la roue
le volant

[A]
Photocopy Master 16.3 p.153

There is quite a lot of vocabulary which needs to be introduced before work on the block begins. Use the Photocopy Master 16.3 to do this. It does not have any language on it so run through it first, identifying the various parts of the car. If you then photocopy it and give it to students in pairs they can learn and test each other as they have the list of vocabulary in the Student Book.

[B] ((•))
Activity 1

Student Book p.182
When you have done the activity in the way suggested, ask a few questions in French about the situation.

T: *Quel est le problème? Que va-t-il faire? Il va mettre combien de temps? Où est la roue?*

[C] ((•))
Activity 2

Student Book p.182
Students can work in pairs to clarify the statements in the book before the tape is heard. Play the tape more

than once to the class until they feel they can answer the questions.

[D]
Activity 3   Quiz

Student Book p.183
You may like to give students the task of reading out the sentences in the quiz. To improve reading skills and help with listening skills, do this task in groups of four. One person has the book and reads the statements and the choices for answers. The others choose the appropriate answer.

[E]
Activity 4   Vous y êtes?

Student Book p.182
Students can work these out in pairs before class checking takes place.

[F]
Activity 5   Allez-y!

Student Book p.182
This role play can be acted out by students. You could give the language of the mechanic on a worksheet or on the OHP for the student who facilitates the role play.

S1: Alors, madame/monsieur, qu'est-ce qui ne va pas?
S2: Ah. C'est peut-être la batterie.
S1: Vous pouvez soulever le capot? Je vais regarder ça.
S2: Je ne sais pas. Revenez dans une heure.

[G]
Points de repère

Student Book p.182
Encourage students to check what they have learned in this unit by testing each other in pairs. They can then record their achievements by filling in the grid provided.

UNITÉ 17 LANGUES ET TRAVAIL

Les jobs d'été

Language

un(e) animateur/trice
aucune formation
une boîte de nuit
un(e) caissier/caissière
la cueillette
cueillir (les choux)
les déménagements
gagner
un organisme d'assistance
payé à l'heure
un permis de conduire
un pourboire
un receveur d'autoroute
la rémunération
le Smic (Salaire minimum interprofessionnel de croissance)
toucher (de l'argent)
les vendanges

[A]
Reading texts

Student Book p.190
The unit opens with reading texts. These are quite extensive and it is best therefore to deal with them in stages. Take one section at a time and ask students to study each one in pairs. Alternatively, you could allocate one section to each pair. As you go through the language, encourage others to ask for clarification of vocabulary (in French). The amount of time spent doing this may be influenced by the overall age range of the students.

You could also ask the students to imagine that they are doing the particular job in the extract being studied and then ask a few questions about what it is like. Explain *Smic*, which is *le Salaire minimum interprofessionnel de croissance*.

Some examples are given here:

1. Déménagements (et rondes de nuit)
Vous gagnez combien? / Vous êtes bien payé(e)?
Vous avez le permis de conduire?
Le travail vous plaît?
Vous travaillez seul?

2. Vendanges et cueillettes
Quand commencez-vous?
Qu'est-ce que vous cueillez?
Les heures de travail sont longues?
Vous commencez à quelle heure?
Vous pouvez commencer à partir de quel âge?

3. Animateurs de centres de vacances
Vous travaillez où?
Vous travaillez avec un groupe d'enfants de quel âge?
Qu'est-ce que vous faites exactement?
Vous êtes logé(e)?
Faut-il une formation?

4. Restauration et hôtellerie
Où travaillez-vous?
Que faites-vous?
Vous gagnez beaucoup?
Et les pourboires?

5. Parcs de loisirs
Que faites-vous?
Quel est l'âge minimum?
Les heures de travail...?
Vous travaillez seul?
Faut-il parler une langue étrangère? Laquelle?

6. Hypermarchés ou épiceries
Vous travaillez dans quelle sorte de magasin?
Vous travaillez en équipe?
Le salaire?

7. Garages
Le salaire?
Vous gagnez des pourboires?
Quel genre de personne devrait se présenter pour le poste de pompiste?

8. Emplois de bureau
Vous travaillez où?
Vous faites quoi?
Vous parlez une langue étrangère?
En quoi consiste le travail pour un organisme d'assistance?

[B]
Activities 1 and 2

Student Book p.191
These activities can be worked on by students in pairs and then reported back. You might like to prepare an answer grid on OHP in advance to speed this up.

[C] ((·))
Activity 3

Student Book p.191
The class should be able to answer these questions after they have heard the recording once. Check the answers with them by going through the tape again.

[D] ((·))
Activity 4

Student Book p.191
Depending on the level of your students, this activity could be done together by playing the tape once or twice only. Weaker students would benefit from a choice of words on the OHP/board to use for the gap-fill activity. These words should also include some redundant vocabulary.

[E]
Activity 5

Student Book p.191
This role play can be done in pairs and then opened out to include other jobs. Hélène's questions could remain largely the same. Allow preparation time and adequate time for pairs to act out their new roles. Alternatively, pairs could go out of the room and record their interviews on tape. Their recordings can then be used for further listening practice for the rest of the class.

Les stages en entreprise

Language

accueillir
la bureautique
le chiffre d'affaires
la durée
effectuer
une facture
gentil(le)
LEA, Langues étrangères appliquées
une licence
la main-d'œuvre
une maîtrise
la motoculture de plaisance
un ordinateur
un PDG, président-directeur général
Ça t'a plu?
la pub, la publicité
réceptionner
rémunéré(e)
le secrétariat
un(e) stagiaire

la traduction
un(e) tuteur/tutrice

[A]
Préparation

Revise vocabulary from Unit 13 on work and training.

[B] ((·))
Activity 1

Student Book p.192
Introduce this block by playing the tape to the class and inviting them to note down any key French words which they recognise (even if they don't know the meaning). Write these up and explain meanings in French if need be. After this, ask students to look at the questions in Activity 1 and again, encourage them to ask (in French) for clarification of any unknown words. Play the tape again so that the questions can be answered. When you have checked the answers with the class you can go on to exploit the tape further. This can be done by asking the class to imagine that they are Monsieur Hanocq and then asking them about the company and the reception of the *stagiaires*. They can suggest what the *stagiaires* may do while in the company.

[C] ((·))
Activity 2

Student Book p.192
This activity can be worked on in pairs by the students. It provides consolidation for the language of the work place.

[D]
Job interviews

To extend the language from Activity 2, invite each pair of students to make up three or four questions that a potential *stagiaire* might want to ask Monsieur Hanocq: *Que fait l'entreprise? Quelles sont les heures de travail?* Go over their suggestions together. A challenging extension would then be for the class to carry out interviews, either based on Monsieur Hanocq or on any of the previous job specifications.

[E]
Activity 4

Student Book p.193
Go through the adverts with the students. The qualifications mentioned are: *DEUG – Diplôme d'études universitaires générales, BTS – Brevet de technicien supérieur, LEA – Langues étrangères appliquées.* When you have been through the adverts, ask the class to match up the students to jobs, justifying their selections.

[F] ((·))
Activity 5

Student Book p.193
This activity can be made more difficult if you write up each incomplete statement on the OHP/board and omit the options. Students do not look in their book. When students note their answers in French, the spelling should be ignored. However, when the answers are checked against the Student Book, the spellings should be examined and discussed.

Le télétravail

Language

en avoir assez/marre de
l'archivage
la comptabilité
un(e) comptable
concilier
craquer
gagner sa vie
le graphisme
grimper
installation informatique
la prise en charge
la Sofres

[A]
Coping with an extended reading passage
Worksheet 17.1 p.154

Here are some suggestions for getting to grips with a longer text. Students could work in small groups and the text is provided on the worksheet so students can write on it if required.
* Look at the title of the article and the sub-headings – do they give any clues to the general meaning?
* Students should realise that they can't feasibly look up every word as it would take forever. Instead, they should go through the text, one sentence at a time, picking out the words they know and underlining those they don't. They should then see if they can piece together a general understanding of the meaning. At the end of a paragraph, they should go back over that whole section before moving on to the next paragraph.
* If students reach the point where they really can't make sense of a sentence, get them to try and pick out two or three words that look key to the meaning. These will generally be nouns or verbs. If something looks like an English word, they should assume at this stage that the meanings are similar.

[B]
Activity 1

Student Book p.194
Once students have been through the whole text, they can do this activity. This will help them to focus on the main points and will confirm how well they have understood the gist of the text.

Students can now go back over the text in more detail to see if there are any phrases or sections they still don't understand or they misinterpreted on their first reading. They should try to find out where they went wrong and now is the time to look up further words in the glossary or a dictionary. They should ask for help if necessary and should not leave the reading passage with words not cleared up. They should be aware, however, that they can still get the gist of the text without having to understand every word.

[C]
Tips for learners

The strategies given in [A] and [B] can be used for any reading text in French. Students should be encouraged to read as much French as they can. Research suggests that it is the most effective way to widen vocabulary.

[D]
Activity 2

Student Book p.194
Ask students to read the text and then offer some true/false statements for them to correct: *Elle est secrétaire. Elle travaille dans un supermarché. Son employeur était pour le télétravail. Elle n'a pas d'enfants. Le désavantage est qu'elle paie les factures de télécommunications.* This gives students practice in shifting from *je* to *elle*. They can then write up their answers to the questions, either in class or at home.

[E]
Extending and practising

At this stage, students could compile lists of the advantages and disadvantages of home working for any job or their own job. These arguments should be prepared to be presented to their boss/the class.

[F]
Activity 3

Student Book p.195
This activity can be done using the groundwork students have done in [E] above. You might extend the scenario in the Student Book by asking the class to imagine their case for home working has been turned down by their boss. Students take the part of employer and employee and try to simulate the conversation in pairs. Allow others to join in with helpful suggestions.

UNITÉ 18 VACANCES

Le tourisme vert

Language

un canal (pl. les canaux)
le canoë-kayak
en cas de dommage
un chemin pédestre
l'escalade
s'étendre
facile
une façon
une ferme
les gens du cru
un gîte
insolite
une randonnée à cheval
une roulotte
la spéléo(logie)
le tourisme vert

[A]
Preparation

It might be useful to revise leisure vocabulary with students before they start this unit.

[B]
Reading for information

Student Book p.199
Study the information on canal holidays. Questions can be asked about the map: *Où se trouve Epinal? Par quelles villes passe le grand canal d'Alsace?* Students can obtain information from you about the price and details of hiring a canal boat. They should close their books for this and then seek the information as though enquiring at an agency, using the cues suggested:

Les prix selon les saisons.
Les prix par semaine...
La capacité des bateaux.
Les possibilités de location.
Problèmes de navigation pour débutants.

[C] «»)
Activities 1 and 2

Student Book p.198
These can be done as class activities. The more technical vocabulary might need discussing first of all.

[D]
Activity 5

Student Book p.198
This should be done in pairs with one student having the doubts expressed in the activity and the other reassuring him/her. Students doing the reassuring can assume either the role of a friend who is experienced in canal boating or someone at an agency. Before this is attempted you may like to go through it in the way suggested but with the whole class, so that they hear how to formulate statements or questions and receive ideas about responding.

Les gîtes de France

[A]
Activity 1

Student Book p.200
Study the short texts and then ask students to do the activity, asking them to justify their reasons for selecting the different types of accommodation for different people. This will involve them in saying, *parce qu'il aime...*

[B]
Tackling the text

Student Book p.200
Use the article about gîtes to teach students how to pick out the main points of an article and write a brief summary in French or a list of recommendations for prospective clients:

Pour devenir l'hôte(sse) idéal(e), vous devez...
* avoir un grand appartement/une grande maison
* vous occuper du ménage...
* préparer le petit déjeuner.
Vous devez aussi...
* aimer la conversation
* avoir le sens de l'hospitalité.

Once you have completed this, as a class or in groups, the students will have no problem doing the tasks in their books.

[C] ((•))
Activity 4

Student Book p.201
This tape is not very difficult and the activity could be attempted at first listening if you wish. Check the answers by going through the tape again. When you have done this you could ask the class to tell you as much as possible about the gîte as though they had stayed there and were describing it to a friend.

[D] ((•))
Activity 5

Student Book p.201
Treat this activity in a similar way to that suggested above. The information contained in it can be used as a basis for a description of how a holiday was spent, what it was like, what the locality provided, etc.

Au bord de la mer

Language

un cotre groisillon
au départ de
un îlot
au large des côtes vendéennes
une navette
la nidification
profiter de
un sentier balisé
un thonier
une traversée

[A] ((•))
Introduction
Worksheet 18.1 p.154

The worksheet can be given to the class to help them become familiar with the material.

[B]
Activities 1 and 2

Student Book p.203
These can now be done in pairs or small groups.

[C]
Activity 3

Student Book p.203
This activity could be done as a whole class activity giving reading and pronunciation practice to students. Invite students to read out the passages. Others can suggest islands that would suit them. Alternatively, students can work in groups of three or four. One student reads a statement and the rest are only allowed to look at the information about the islands. They can ask for repetition and must then select the island.

[D]
Pairwork

Put the names of the islands on the OHP/board. Students work in pairs and ask their partner questions about a particular island. The partner uses the book to provide information as though he or she is at the tourist office.

UNITÉ 19 CULTURE: SÉJOUR À PARIS

Où dormir? Où manger?

Language

une auberge de jeunesse
un déjeuner d'affaires
draps fournis
la fermeture
garer
goûter à
l'hébergement
inclus
un lavabo

[A]

Preparation

Student Book p.206
Read the introduction with the students. As well as ensuring comprehension, use it for practice in expressing likes, dislikes and preferences: *Vous aimez les grands hôtels de luxe? Vous avez fait du camping? Qu'est-ce que vous préférez, un grand hôtel ou un petit hôtel familial? Vous connaissez les auberges de jeunesse?*

[B]

Activity 1   Auberge d'Artagnan

Student Book p.207
Students will need to read the realia with care in order to find the answers. Have them indicate where in the material they have found the information (that which tells them what is not available as well as what is).

Once students have found answers and fed them back, you might use the six items given for quick practice in questioning. Individuals phone the *Auberge d'Artagnan* and have short conversations like this:

S1: *Auberge d'Artagnan, bonjour.*
S2: *Bonjour monsieur/madame. Est-ce qu'il y a des chambres avec télévision, s'il vous plaît?*
S1: *Oui, monsieur/madame, dans quarante de nos chambres pour deux personnes.*
S2: *Merci, monsieur/madame.*

This could then lead to pair practice, with one student phoning and putting all six questions, and the other student, the receptionist, supplying the information which students have found and confirmed. They could also enquire about prices of rooms and facilities.

[C] ((•))

Activity 2   Camping du Bois de Boulogne

Student Book p.207
Note that the answers to these questions are not all simple *oui/non: Il y a un restaurant, mais nous ne savons pas si c'est un très bon restaurant! On peut aller à Paris en bus entre les mois d'avril et octobre.*

When students have done the exercise as set, and some time has elapsed, ask them to tell you in French where the hostel and the campsites are, and what facilities are available. The motivation is apparently: Can you **remember**? but in fact you are having them re-use some of the useful language of this unit.

[D]

Activity 3   Liste des restaurants

Student Book p.207
The activity is a straightforward one. When students have done it and you have checked answers, read through the adverts with them pointing out (or have them try to tell you) items of interest not covered in the activity – What is a *kir*? What is the significance of *offert*? What is the difference between *une salade* and *une salade composée*? What is *le terroir*?

[E] ((•))

Activity 4   Cue Cards 19.1 p.155

Student Book p.207
Use the cue cards to practise phone bookings. A model dialogue is given below.

B: *Ici le camping, bonjour.*
A: *Ah, bonjour, madame. Je voudrais réserver un emplacement, s'il vous plaît.*
B: *Oui. C'est pour quand?*
A: *C'est pour le cinq juillet... du cinq au huit.*
B: *Trois nuits, alors?*
A: *C'est cela.*
B: *Et vous avez une tente, une caravane...?*
A: *Une tente. Une tente pour deux personnes.*
B: *Deux adultes?*
A: *Deux adultes.*
B: *C'est bon. Votre nom, s'il vous plaît? ...*

Les marchés mode d'emploi

Language

les antiquités
les bijoux
la brocante
les (bonnes) affaires
les épices
fréquenté(e)
marchander
le marché aux puces
les meubles
le mode d'emploi
d'occasion
un oiseau
la philatélie
faire des prix
les puces
le quartier
les rapports
reputé(e) pour

[A]
Activities 1 and 2

Student Book p.209
Read through the introduction with the students and then have them do Activities 1 and 2 by reading the descriptions of the markets on their own.

[B] ((•))
Activity 3

Student Book p.209
Ask students to read through the rubric for Activity 3 and then play the tape. Invite students to make the briefest of notes on the two interviews in French. Then using their notes, students talk about each of the stall holders: *Le premier marchand vend des... Il travaille de... à... Il travaille au marché depuis... Il aime bien... En général, ses clients sont de...*

[C] ((•))
Activities 4 and 5

Student Book p.209
Use the short utterances as models for students to imitate.

[D] ((•))
Activity 6
Cue Cards 19.2 p.155

Student Book p.209
In preparation for this tape about a visit to the *marché d'Aligre*, make up some paragraphs about visits you have made to two or three of the other markets. Either read them aloud or write them on the board/OHP. Students make notes of what they hear/read, and then decide which market you visited.

T: *Alors, moi je suis allée au marché un samedi matin. C'était vraiment bien! J'ai acheté un pull d'occasion pour mon mari, et une jupe verte pour moi. J'ai acheté également de la coriandre et du cumin. J'ai admiré l'artisanat africain – masques et sculptures en bois... mais je n'en ai pas acheté.*

Later, they feed back from their notes the narrative of your visit(s).

Students can use the cue cards to make dialogues with each other about a trip to a market. If required, they can then write a postcard about a visit to *marché d'Aligre*. You might like to write an example up for them first on the board/OHP.

A travers Paris

Language

l'assurance
autrefois
connu(e)
une croisière
la location
une nocturne
A voir!

[A] ((•))
Activity 1

Student Book p.210
Play the tape and have students complete the activity. This is a good point in the course to pull together the adverbs: *souvent, rarement, parfois, peu, avant, autrefois, généralement, aujourd'hui*, and to add a few more: *régulièrement, de temps en temps...*

Encourage students to use some of them as you use the first activity as a basis for asking them about their own leisure activities – revising and building on what was done in Unit 10.

[B]
Activity 2   Canal Saint-Martin

Student Book p.211
This can usefully be done in pairs. Both students read the leaflet, then one of them covers up the questions and looks only at the leaflet. The second student asks the questions.

[C]
Activities 3 and 4

Student Book p.211
Have students indicate which part of the realia allows them to decide on their answers. The *vélo* information could easily be used as a basis for reporting on past events: *Moi, j'ai fait une excursion à vélo. Le rendez-vous à Paris vélo était à vingt et une heures. La promenade a duré environ trois heures. Nous avons longé les quais de la Seine, nous avons vu l'Assemblée nationale, la tour Eiffel... J'ai loué un beau vélo et c'était relativement peu cher – 180 francs tout compris.*

You might say such a paragraph aloud, then ask students to give the same information orally. They could then write it up for homework. Students could work in pairs or small groups to plan their own cycling tour. They then report back to the class who have to follow the route on maps. This allows students to choose their own itinerary and makes the realia more meaningful for them.

[D]
Activity 5
Photocopy Master 19.3 p.156

Student Book p.211
Have students complete the diary pages on the photocopy master with the things they choose to do on their weekend in Paris.

Once they have completed the diary entries, they can work in pairs, each taking a turn at the role of the Parisian friend. You can add an extra dimension for strong students by having the Parisian friend react to the proposals: *Chouette! Bonne idée! Les touristes n'y vont pas, en général...* and give advice: *Oui, mais vas-y (plutôt) samedi matin...*

After this pairwork, students can use exactly the same diary entries to give an oral or written account of what they actually **did** on their weekend in Paris: *Je suis arrivé vendredi soir. Je suis descendu dans un petit hôtel près de la Gare du Nord. Samedi matin, je suis allé au marché aux puces... j'ai acheté de l'artisanat africain. Samedi après-midi, je suis allé à la tour Eiffel. Il faut voir la tour, n'est-ce pas?*

As in this example, they should be encouraged to add details – what they did does not match exactly what they intended to do, etc. and they should add reactions to what they did: *J'ai très bien mangé! La promenade à vélo, c'était vraiment bien. J'ai aimé la tour Eiffel, mais quel monde!*

Students might then like to write a postcard home about their visit.

UNITÉ 20 LES FRANCOPHONES

On y parle français

Language

apprendre
une communauté francophone
un(e) francophone
une langue étrangère
une langue maternelle
une langue officielle
les palmarès
sans statut particulier

[A]
Class quiz

This unit is essentially cultural in content, based on a number of reading activities. Have students predict the answers to the first set of questions before they read the text. This could be done as a team activity with the students using their own general knowledge to gain points for their team. You, or a student with the texts, can tell them if they are right or not.

Europe francophone

Language

autonome
bilingue
enceinte
enclavé(e)
une espèce de
un évêque
le flamand
le navet
le pot-au-feu
la poule

[A]
Activities 1 and 2

Student Book p.216
Use the same technique for this section of the unit as for the first section.

[B] ((◦))
Activity 3

Student Book p.216
Play the tape in the two parts indicated in the Student Book. Once students have ticked the responses and checked that their answers are correct, give them a few minutes to prepare and then ask them, in French, to recall all they can about Christel Verhoye and her opinions.

[C]
Talking about regions

Distribute the regions/countries described in the text among the students. After a few minutes' reading and preparation, have them give short presentations of the part of the world they have been reading about. They should speak from memory or from very brief notes.

La France dans le monde

Language

les activités nautiques
un bateau à fond de verre
la chaleur
un chef-lieu
le créole
un cyclone
le dépaysement
la France métropolitaine
une grotte
un lac souterrain
un mélange
d'outre-mer
le patois
un piment
le riz
un sentier de grande randonnée
la superficie
les tarifs aériens
un volcan

[A]
Activity 1

Student Book p.218
Do the activity as set. Then inform students you are

going to ask them to recall the information (and language) without reading it, using the brief notes below on the OHP/board:

> Destination d'hiver
>
> Premier séjour
>
> Difficile de choisir

[B]
Activity 2
Photocopy Master 20.1 p.156

Student Book p.218
Use the pictures from the photocopy master to make flashcards. These will help students recall the vocabulary, once they have found it in the texts.

Use pairs of flashcards and ask: *Qu'est-ce que vous allez faire à...?* Students answer in the same future tense: *Je vais faire du cheval et je vais faire des promenades en bateau.*

At another time, use the same flashcards to prompt use of the perfect tense: *Qu'est-ce que vous avez fait à...? Je suis allé(e) à la pêche et j'ai fait des randonnées (à pied).* If you want to include further leisure pursuits, you could use Choice Framework 10.1 on p.137.

[C]
Activities 3 and 4

Student Book pp.218–219
Use the technique described in [A]. In Activity 4, students can produce sentences such as: *Je voudrais voir une grotte avec un lac souterrain. Je vais à...*

[D]
Activity 6

Student Book p.219
Do the activity in pairs, with all students taking each role in turn. You can easily extend this activity, using much of the same language and other items too, by asking students to choose a holiday destination, perhaps from a given list, and inviting others to play the role of a French-speaking friend who does not know about the resorts:

Skegness – C'est où exactement? Tu y vas à quel moment de l'année? Pourquoi? Qu'est-ce qu'il y a à faire?

La Barbade? Blackpool? Dingle? Édimbourg? St Ives? Le sud de l'Espagne?

ASSESSMENT UNIT 11-20

The assessments

As with the assessment unit for units 1–10, these assessments cover speaking, listening, reading and writing and are communicative rather than grammatical. The reading and writing assessments could be done by students in their own time if they wish, but the listening and speaking need to be carried out in class. There is no set time limit for any of the assessments. They should be completed without reference works. Prepare students for the assessments by explaining what they will cover, telling them in advance when they will be and how their performances will be judged. Two main points to underline are:
* in speaking assessments, students will be judged first and foremost on their ability to seek and receive communicative messages, and **secondarily** by the quality of language used.
* in reading and listening assessments, students should not expect to score 100%. This reflects real life.
Most of the assessments can be marked by the students themselves if you provide the mark scheme, but the oral assessments do require someone to listen to the exchanges and record marks at that time. Marking schemes are provided after the cue cards.

Oral assessments

As with the first assessment unit, there is a range of oral tasks. All involve using cue cards. As assessor, you will need a copy of the mark sheet on which you can note the achievement of the task, i.e. that the appropriate pieces of information have been sought or conveyed. Students may well ask for things to be spelled out and for repetition, etc. Doing these well counts towards the mark awarded for quality of French.
There are four tasks provided: an extended interview between French-speakers role-played by students in pairs, and three transactions, two of which involve interpreting for a monolingual. Students may perform the first assessment as two separate interviews or conduct an interactive conversation.

1. Extended interview – giving and seeking information and attitudes

Working with another student, find out his/her corresponding details below, by asking appropriate questions. (e.g. Your name is given, so to find out

her/his name, you can ask: *Comment vous appelez-vous?*) Make a note of what your partner tells you in any form you wish. There are ten items of information to convey.

Student A	Student B
Rachid (f) ou Haroun Nadir	*Fatima (f) ou Osman Nur*
Né(e): Alg	*Né(e): Oran*
Domicile actuel: Paris	*Domicile actuel: Marseille*
Travail actuel: secrétaire	*Travail actuel: journaliste*
Jobs passés: 5 ans, serveur (-euse) dans un magasin	*Jobs passés: 1 an, prof*
Langues: français, arabe	*Langues: français*
Loisirs: tennis, théâtre	*Loisirs: cinéma, photos*
Vacances: montagne (air baignade, enfants)	*Vacances: mer (air frais, calme, frais, repos)*
Plats préférés: couscous, glace café	*Plats préférés: steack frites, pain aux olives*

MARK SCHEMES
1 point for asking about or giving the following items:
- birth-place
- present address
- present job
- past job(s)
- time spent on that job
- languages spoken
- leisure activities
- holiday preferences
- reasons for these
- food: favourite dishes

Items conveyed: ..../10
Quality of French: ..../10
Total: ..../20

2. Ordering a meal

You and a partner are in a restaurant. Your partner speaks little or no French. (Ensure that your partner understands that she/he is to pretend to be less competent than he/she really is in understanding French. This role is not assessed.) Order a meal for the two of you from your tutor who is the waiter/waitress.

Restaurant des Pyrénées

Menu à 65F	Menu à 100 F
ou: Salade de tomates	ou: Sardines fraîches
ou: Jambon de pays	grillées
	ou: Quiche lorraine
ou: Escalope de dinde	ou: Pizza
ou: Steack	
Frites ou haricots verts	ou: Couscous
	ou: Coq au vin/
Fromage ou dessert	frites/haricots verts
	Plateau de fromages
	Tarte tatin
	Mousse au chocolat
	Pâtisserie maison

MARK SCHEMES

2 points for each of the following items:
which menu partner requires
telling monolingual what the first courses are
ordering a first course
telling monolingual what the main courses are
ordering a main course
clarifying for monolingual what vegetables are required/available
saying whether cheese or dessert is required (menu 1) **OR** dealing with the dessert choice (menu 2).

Items conveyed: ..../14
Quality of French: ..../16
Total:.../30

3. A la pharmacie

Work with a partner and hold a dialogue at the chemist's using the cues provided below. Your tutor is the chemist.

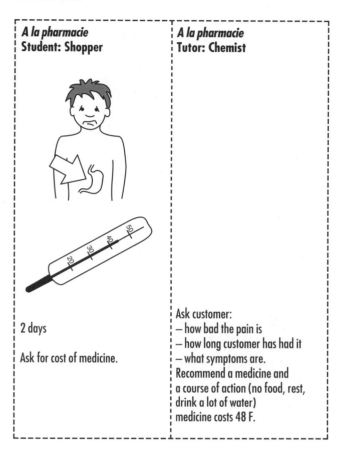

A la pharmacie Student: Shopper	A la pharmacie Tutor: Chemist
2 days Ask for cost of medicine.	Ask customer: – how bad the pain is – how long customer has had it – what symptoms are. Recommend a medicine and a course of action (no food, rest, drink a lot of water) medicine costs 48 F.

MARK SCHEMES

2 points each for telling chemist:
stomach ache
temperature
how long the problem has been there
ask cost of medicine
Greetings are expected (*Bonjour, madame/monsieur; au revoir...*) but not scored on this occasion.

Items conveyed: ..../8
Quality of French:../7
Total:.../15

4. Buying clothes/shoes

The tutor plays the part of the shop assistant. In general, you have that which the customer (the student) wants. However, put in one 'joker' such as you have the right shirt in the wrong colour, or it is a lot more expensive than the customer wants to pay. Student B plays the part of an English-speaking monolingual. (Ensure that this person understands that she/he is to pretend to be less competent than he/she really is in understanding French. This role is not assessed.)

MARK SCHEMES

Buying clothes: 1 point each for:
    partner wants shirt for self
    partner wants T-shirt for daughter
    size of adult shirt
    striped
    colours required
    small T-shirt
    cotton
    colours
2 points for dealing with the 'joker'
Items conveyed (+ joker): ..../10
Quality of French: ..../10
Total: ..../20

Buying shoes: 1 point each for:
    saying shoes seen in window
    stating colour requirements
    giving size required
    saying partner would like to try shoes on
    dealing satisfactorily with payment
    2 points for dealing with the 'joker'
Items conveyed (+ joker): ..../7
Quality of French: ..../5
Total: ..../12

Listening assessments

The tapescripts for the listening assessments are printed below. If possible, find a French native speaker who will present the information in the text. He/she could record it on cassette. If you cannot manage this, get to know the content of the text well and perform it yourself. Make the pace of delivery as natural as you can, without hurrying. It will be most natural if you build in some repetitions.

Tapescript 1

Aujourd'hui, j'habite la Bretagne, tout près de Rennes. Rennes, c'est une grande ville, alors, pour les loisirs, je peux pratiquer toutes sortes d'activités: le tennis, le bowling, le patinage... Puis, en été, on n'est pas loin de la mer, et j'aime bien me baigner. Je ne suis plus très jeune, et les activités comme la planche à voile ne me tentent pas!
Le climat est très doux: il ne fait pas très froid en hiver, mais il ne fait pas trop chaud en été. Le seul problème, c'est qu'il pleut beaucoup... enfin, plus que dans l'est.
Avant, j'habitais dans les Pyrénées, dans les environs de Bagnères de Bigorre. Là, le climat, c'est un climat de montagne: froid en hiver, très chaud en été, avec pas mal d'orages. Et puis, là-bas, les étés sont courts. Quand j'habitais là-bas, j'étais jeune, et j'adorais la montagne; l'été, je faisais de l'escalade, je faisais des randonnées à pied... puis en hiver c'était le ski. J'en faisais à la Mongie, tout près de là où j'habitais. C'était magnifique.

Tapescript 2

L'année dernière, j'ai passé des vacances magnifiques. On est parti en famille en Corse. Nous sommes descendus dans un petit hôtel près de Bastia. L'hôtel était simple, mais correct, et la cuisine excellente. Il a fait beau pendant les quinze jours que nous avons passés en Corse. Nous avons loué une voiture et nous avons pu visiter l'intérieur, qui est très montagneux, avec des villages très isolés. Puis, sur la côte, nous avons profité des plages: (mon mari) ma femme a fait de la planche à voile, et moi, j'ai fait de la pêche. C'était reposant comme tout!
Contraste avec des vacances que j'ai faites dans les années 80, en 85, plus exactement. Ma femme et moi, nous avons campé dans le Jura, près de Champagnole. C'est très joli, par là. Le problème, c'est qu'il a plu presque tous les jours. On a visité des églises, des châteaux, mais pour la marche à pied, que nous aimons beaucoup, ou pour le tennis, nous en avons fait très peu. Se promener en montagne sous la pluie, ce n'est pas mon rêve, hein?

1. Weather and leisure

Listen to someone talking about how things used to be, and how things are now, in terms of climates experienced and their leisure activities. Note information (in English) on the proforma below.

	AVANT	A PRESENT
Région/Climat:		....
....	....	
....		
....		
Activités:		
....		
....		
....		

MARK SCHEMES
1 point for each of the following:

BRITTANY

tennis	ten pin bowling
skating	bathing (sea-side)
temperate climate	mild winters
coolish summers	much rain

PYRÉNÉES

cold winters	short wet summers
storms	rock climbing
walking	skiing

Total: ..../16

2. Travels

Listen and note information (in English) on the proforma below.

```
VACANCES 94
– destination: .........................................
– hébergement: ......................................
– activités:..............................................
...............................................................
– bilan: ..................................................

VACANCES 85
– destination: .........................................
– hébergement: ......................................
– activités:..............................................
...............................................................
– bilan: ..................................................
```

MARK SCHEMES
1 point each for these items entered under the right headings:

CORSICA

- small hotel
- motoring (hire car)
- visit mountains (interior)
- seaside
- self fished
- spouse did windsurfing
- restful
- very successful (great, etc.)

JURA

- camping
- rain
- churches and castles
- rotten (not very successful, etc.)

Total:../14

Reading assessments

As with the first assessment unit, ensure that students understand exactly what is required of them. Remind them about reading strategies and making sensible guesses at things they have not seen.

1. Dieppe et les Anglais

A neighbour picked up a brochure with this page in it, on their way through Dieppe. Their French is not very good and they think the page is about the way English tourists are 'taking over the town'. Read the text carefully and write the answers to the questions below, in English.

> *Deux excellents ouvrages de Sylvia Packenham retracent l'histoire de la colonie britannique qui se fixe à Dieppe au XIXe siècle et jusqu'en 1939.*
> *Dieppe a été, au XIXe siècle, une ville quasi anglaise. Lord Salisbury à Puys, les Hosier à Dieppe (liés à Churchill), Beardsley, Ruskin, Oscar Wilde et bien d'autres ont vécu là.*
> *Le peintre Jacques Emile Blanche, parisien qui avait épousé une anglaise, avait choisi Dieppe, à mi-chemin entre Paris et Londres où il avait aussi un atelier. Il a fait beaucoup pour mettre notre ville à la mode.*
> *Il y avait trois pensions d'éducation, deux églises anglicanes, des épiceries, des pharmacies anglaises. Chaque commerçant était fier de porter sur sa vitrine: English spoken.*
> *Et maintenant? La colonie anglaise est bien réduite mais de nouveaux liens se tissent avec Brighton, avec le Leicestershire, les excursions se multiplient. Et grâce à la ligne Dieppe-Newhaven, non seulement les visites des Britanniques à Dieppe, mais des échanges franco-britanniques continueront à se développer.*

The neighbour would like to know:

1. how far they are right

2. why Oscar Wilde is mentioned

3. why 1939 is mentioned

4. who Jacques Emile Blanche was

5. why Leicestershire is mentioned

6. whether the text says that all the people in Dieppe speak English

7. why Newhaven-Dieppe is mentioned

MARK SCHEMES

2 points for each answer which is fully correct. 1 point is awarded for answers which tell part of the truth.

1. They are NOT right; the article is about the way English people settled in and around Dieppe.
2. Because he lived in Dieppe for some time.
3 Because it marked the end of Dieppe as a fashionable spot for upper class/artistic British people.
4. He was a Parisian artist who married an English woman and settled in Dieppe. He helped make Dieppe fashionable among the British.
5. Because links are developing between Dieppe and Leicestershire, among other places.
6. No. It says that in the heyday of Dieppe as a British resort, shopkeepers were proud to put that notice in their shops.
7. The Newhaven-Dieppe ferry service is seen as the means by which visits by British tourists, and also exchange visits between the two countries, will grow in the future.

Total: ..../14

Written assessments

1. Careers

Complete these sentences so that they make sense.

1. *J'ai travaillé d'abord dans les cuisines, puis j'ai fait le service. Maintenant, je suis _____ de la gestion du restaurant.*

2. *Moi, je travaille chez Oxynor. Je suis à la direction commerciale et je m'occupe de la _____ des produits.*

3. *Moi, je voudrais faire des _____ de photographie, pour devenir photographe.*

4. *Moi, j'ai fait une _____ de voyagiste. J'ai fait cela dans une école de tourisme à Paris.*

5. *Moi, j'ai fait une licence de langues étrangères appliquées: trois ans d'études, avec un _____ pratique en industrie.*

6. *Moi, je suis à la retraite. J'ai beaucoup d'activités. Je ne m' _____ jamais.*

7. *Je n'ai pas à me déplacer pour mon travail: je fais du secrétariat à _____.*

8. *Madame Simon n'est pas là? Elle pourrait me _____ plus tard, peut-être?*

9. *Monsieur Blanc? Attendez, je vous le passe... ah, je regrette, son poste est _____*

10. *Je n'ai pas votre adresse, ni votre numéro. Vous pouvez me donner vos _____ ?*

MARK SCHEMES

1 point for each of the following, if in your judgment it is intelligible to a sympathetic native reader.

1. *responsable*	2. *vente*
3. *études*	4. *formation*
5. *stage*	6. *ennuie*
7. *domicile*	8. *rappeler*
9. *occupé*	10. *coordonnées*

Total:../10

2. Finding the French

What do you say in French for the following situations?

1. You are in the swimming pool and your French friends arrive. You want them to join you and the water's warm. What do you say?

....

2. You've just had a wonderful day out. A French friend asks you how it went. What do you say?

....

3. A French visitor tells you that she has been to Africa. Ask her whether she went to Senegal.

....

4. Your French friend asks you how the trip to London went. Your train was late, it rained all day and the food was awful. Can you tell her/him what you thought of it, in a single word?

....

5. Your car has a puncture. You take it to be mended. You want to know if it will take long. How will you ask that question?

....

6. You're in a shop and have seen some trousers you like. You'd like to try them on. What do you say?

....

7. You go the confectioner's and buy some chocolates. They're for a friend and you'd like them nicely wrapped. What do you ask?

....

8. In a brasserie, you'd like to know what kind of omelettes they do. What would you ask the waiter?

....

9. Problem – the waiter brings the omelette, but you have no fork. What do you say?

....

10. Your French host offers you a meringue. You decline, saying that you don't like sweet things. What do you say?

....

MARK SCHEMES

2 points each for the following answers (or others which you find acceptable):

    1. *L'eau est bonne/elle est bonne!*
    2. *Magnifique!* (or equivalent)
    3. *Vous êtes allée au Sénégal? (Vous avez visité le Sénégal?)*
    4. *Nul!*
    5. *Ça va être long?*
    6. *Je peux l'essayer?*
    7. *Vous me faites un paquet-cadeau, (s'il vous plaît).*
    8. *Qu'est-ce que vous faites comme omelettes?*
    9. *Je n'ai pas de fourchette.*
    10. *Je n'aime pas les choses sucrées.*

Total:.../20

3. Une carte postale

a) You are in Besançon. You have found a little hotel near the centre. The weather is fine. You are enjoying the food, and sightseeing. Write a postcard to a French friend about it. Don't translate word for word, but mention the same points as are given in the English summary above.

b) You are in Beynac on the Dordogne. You are camping near the river. The weather was good for two days, but it rained for the last three. Food good, though. Write a postcard to a French friend about it, as in a).

MARK SCHEMES

For each postcard, award one point for each item of information which is conveyed such that a sympathetic native reader would understand it. Award up to 6 points for grammatical accuracy: this does not mean deducting a mark for each error. Give marks on the impression you think a native speaker would have of the writer's grasp of the way French works.

    6 items a): Besançon, little hotel, town centre, food good, weather fine, sightseeing good
    6 items (b): Beynac, camping, near river, weather OK for two days, now rain for three, food good

Items a):.../6
Items b):.../6
Grammar:../6
Total:../18

114

Prénom	Nom	Age	Travail
Jean	Moreau	30	sec
Madeleine	Dubois	33	arch
Pascal	Petit	45	étud
Thomas	Thomas	50	jour
Elodie	Durand	56	gar

Elodie Petit	**Madeleine Thomas**	**Sylvie Durand**
45 ans	50 ans	20 ans
sec	arch	étud
née: Grenoble	née: Genève	née: Bruxelles
nat: f	nat: suisse	nat: bel
habite: Paris	habite: Lyon	habite: Ostende
Eric Laurent	**Philippe Petit**	**André Simon**
40 ans	21 ans	55 ans
gar	étud	prof
né: Lyon	né: Lyon	né: Bruxelles
nat: f	nat: f	nat: bel
habite: Lyon	habite: Paris	fabite: Ostende

CUE CARDS 2.1 P.18

Paul	Sylvie	Jack	Maria
23	46	31	36
angl	f	aust	esp
architecte	journaliste	méc	sec
mar – Yvonne	ami – Michel	div	veu
		ami – Babette	ami – Miguel
Yvonne	Michel	Babette	Miguel
âge?	âge?	âge?	âge?
profession?	profession?	profession?	profession?

CUE CARDS 2.2 P.20

André	Sylvie	Raoul	Sandrine
grand-père 68	sœur 15	grand-père 69	mère 42
sœur 20	cousine 2	sœur 27	grand-père 67
tante 44	grand-mère 63	oncle 47	oncle 38
		mère 47	cousine 20

André	Sylvie	Raoul	Sandrine
cousine 22	frère 12	grand-mère 68	oncle 37
frère 19	oncle 35	cousin 19	cousin 21
neveu 1 mois	mère 39	tante 49	neveu 3
		frère 25	grand-mère 68

André	Sylvie	Raoul	Sandrine
cousin 14	tante 32	cousine 27	cousine 25
nièce 34	cousine 3	nièce 3 mois	grand-père 66
sœur 24	grand-père 67	demi-frère 12	sœur 19
			frère 17

André	Sylvie	Raoul	Sandrine
mère 46	cousin 3	oncle 42	père 51
oncle 54	sœur 8	père 57	frère 15
tante 43		sœur 23	cousin 25
			nièce 2 mois

WORKSHEET 2.3 P.20

André	Sylvie	Raoul	Sandrine
12 personnes	11 personnes	14 personnes	16 personnes

Pauline Helt 12 2 fr: Georges, Michel 1 s: Sarah m: Sandra (angl) p: André (f) Marseille	**Laure Balesta** 9 1 fr: Simon 1 s: Carmen m: Lina (it) p: Albert (f) Milan	**Mohamed Hamel** 7 2 fr: Djamel, Hamid 1 s: Hanane m: Marie (f) p: Kader (algé) Sète	**Thierry Charles** 6 1 fr: Frédéric 2 s: Emmanuelle, Juliette m: Astrid (dan) p: Yves (f) Copenhague
Jack Laurent 11 1 fr: Max 1 s: Valérie m: Patricia (f) p: Dennis (amé) New York	**Samuel Lenôtre** 6 1 fr: Paul 1 s: Nathalie m: Anouk (algé) p: Luc (f) Lyon	**Sophie Poirot** 10 1 fr: Daniel 2 s: Marie-Anne, Isabelle m: Christine (f) p: Henri (belg) Paris	**Laurence Béranger** 11 1 fr: Jean-Louis 2 s: Annic, Aurélie m: Stéphanie (can) p: Claude (f) Grenoble

Choisissez un nom...

NOM: ....

Ville	Profession	Nationalité	Status familiale	Pays de naissance	Famille	Age
Paris	mécanicien	hollandais(e)	divorcé(e)	France	mère	1 mois
Dijon	médecin	belge	marié(e)	Italie	père	1 – 100 ans
Djibouti	professeur	français(e)	célibataire	Canada	grand-mère	
Londres	secrétaire	anglais(e)	séparé(e)	Egypte	grand-père	
Montpellier	chauffeur de taxi	japonais(e)	femme	Afrique du Sud	fils	
Genève	architecte	italien(ne)	mari	Suisse	fille	
Berlin	ingénieur	algérien(ne)	ami(e)	Allemagne	cousin(e)	
Madrid		tunisien(ne)	seul(e)	Chine	neveu	
		américain(e)	veuf (-ve)		nièce	
					oncle	
					tante	
					frère	
					sœur	

Complete the following sentences.

1 Jeanne Le Dantec travaille .... secrétaire .... Ford.

2 Jacques Maynard travaille .... mécanicien .... Renault; il travaille .... une usine
.... Boulogne-Billancourt.

3 George Smith travaille .... Ellesmore Port. Il est mécanicien .... Vauxhall.

4 Madeleine Dupont est comptable. Elle .... chez Oxyor, ... Rouen.

5 Evelyne Buanic est .... chez ....

6 Werner Schmidt .... bib .... Il .... dans ....
.... Cologne.

7 Catherine Duclos .... elle .... Paris. Elle ....

8 Fred Robinson ....

CHOICE FRAMEWORK 3.2 P.25

Nom	Travail	Lieu	Commence	Finit	✗✔
Hélène	inf	bur	8 h	18 h 30	✗
Georges	journ	H	12 h	00 h 00	✗
Michel	X	us	8 h	18 h	✔
Marie	vend	école	10 h	23 h	✔
Elodie	65+	bib	14 h	20 h	✔
Chantal	bib	M&S	8 h 30	16 h 30	✗

CUE CARDS 3.3 P.25

Marie-France Moulène
IBM
Paris
sec
8 h 30 – 18 h
✔ ✔

parfois surtout
le matin l'après-midi

Michel Vallet

Paris
bib
9 h – 18 h
✗ ✗

parfois surtout
le matin l'après-midi

Aline Guillaumont

inf
Rouen
22 h – 7 h
✔ ✔

parfois surtout
le matin l'après-midi

Henri Blanc
Garage Peugeot
Clermont F.
méc
8 h – 18 h
✗ ✗

parfois surtout
le matin l'après-midi

Marie Ducreux

Marseille
7 h – 19 h 30
hôtesse d'accueil
✔ ✔

parfois surtout
le matin l'après-midi

Gregory Harrison

inf
Londres
8 h – 16 h
✔ ✔

parfois surtout
le matin l'après-midi

Nom	Travail	Jours de travail	Sorties
Eric	*plombier*	*lmmjv*	*pisc*

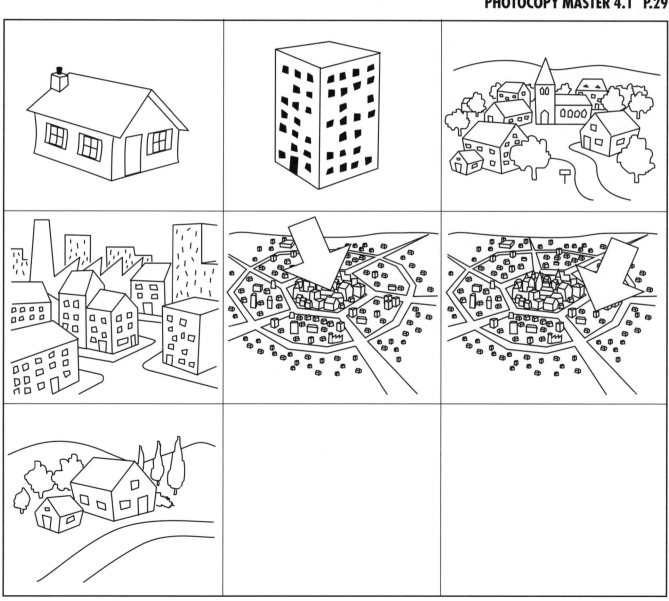

Using the words and sketches given below write ten sentences. One of the portraits should be a fictional account of you. At least one should be about a couple.

Nom?	Domicile	Villes	habiter – où?	travailler – où?/comme?
		Niort	à... km de	banque
		Rennes	campagne	magasin
		Nantes	centre-ville	professeur
		Angers	banlieue	mécanicien
		Villages/Hameaux		
		Augers		
		Crian		
		Blédan		
		Nieron		
		Pitot		

120 **4**

Marcel	habiter	Nantes	ville	centre-ville
Alice	travailler	Rennes	village	
Sandrine		Sizan	grand	
Jacques		Clair	petit	
Adrienne		Marseille	jardin	
Auguste		Amiens	maison	banlieue
Joséphine		Grenoble		village
Marc		Salles		au bord de la mer
M. et Mme Lachèvre		Bordeaux		dans les montagnes
Paul et Laurence		Aret	appartement	
Jeanne et Yves				

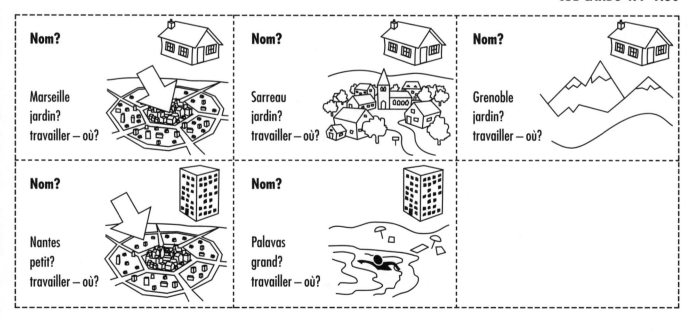

Nom?

Marseille
jardin?
travailler – où?

Nom?

Sarreau
jardin?
travailler – où?

Nom?

Grenoble
jardin?
travailler – où?

Nom?

Nantes
petit?
travailler – où?

Nom?

Palavas
grand?
travailler – où?

A	35	8	55	38	12	**B**	27	14	10	45	31

Lesnevan	Carcassonne	Chambéry	Nozay
quoi? où? dép? où?	quoi? où? dép? où?	quoi? où? dép? où?	quoi? où? dép? où?
St. Etienne quoi? où? dép? où?	**Banon** quoi? où? dép? où?	**Montfaucon** quoi? où? dép? où?	**Vierzon** quoi? où? dép? où?
Pau quoi? où? dép? où?	**Bapaume** quoi? où? dép? où?	**Montfort** quoi? où? dép? où?	**Figeac** quoi? où? dép? où?
Lesnevan village 26 km NE Brest le Finistère (O)	**Carcassonne** ville 92 km E Toulouse l'Aude (S)	**Chambéry** ville moyenne 93 km E Lyon la Savoie (E)	**Nozay** pte ville 41 km N Nantes la Loire-Atlantique (O)
St. Etienne gde ville 45 km SO Lyon la Loire (centre)	**Banon** village 85 km E Avignon la Haute-Provence (SE)	**Montfaucon** village 40 km NO Verdun la Meuse (NE)	**Vierzon** ville 33 km NO Bourges le Cher (centre)
Pau ville 190 km S Bordeaux les Pyrénées-Atlantiques (SO)	**Bapaume** pte ville 47 km NE Amiens le Pas-de-Calais (N)	**Montfort** pte ville 20 km O Rennes l'Ille-et-Vilaine (NO)	**Figeac** pte ville 65 km SO Aurillac le Lot (centre)

André et moi, on habite dans une maison à Presles dans la rue Prince.

C'est la campagne, quoi. C'est une ville. Il y a beaucoup d'arbres et un jardin, et c'est en général très calme. En tout cas, comparé à Paris, c'est très calme.

A Presles, il y a une boulangerie, donc il y a de petits commerces déjà. C'est important. Il y a une boulangerie, deux boucheries, une pharmacie et un supermarché. Il y a quatre garages. C'est énorme pour une ville de 3 400 habitants.

✗✗
Montblazon – ville
grande
trop de bruit/monde
pas de campagne

✔✔
Valan – ville
assez grande
calme
lycée
magasins
près de la campagne

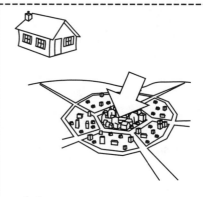

✔✔
Dorton – ville
petite
agréable
musée
cinéma, restaurants

✔✔
Sève – village
restaurant
cinéma
près de la ville
calme

✔✔
Noriot – ville
moyenne
agréable/animée
beaucoup de monde
de magasins

✗✗
Masard – hameau
pas de cinéma/restaurant/café/magasins
loin de la ville

CUE CARDS 5.1 P.36

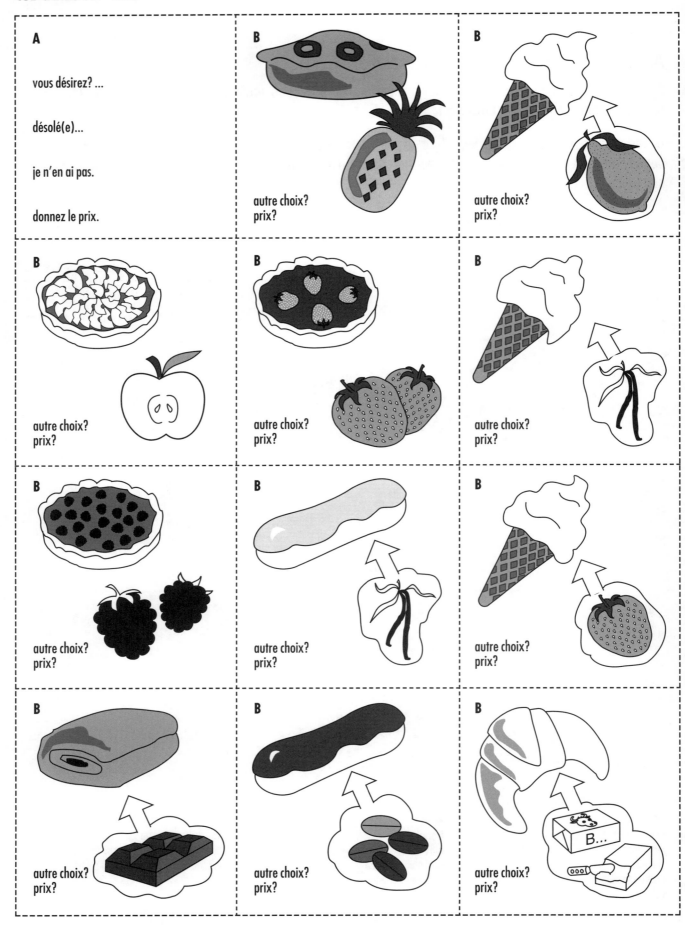

A

vous désirez? ...

désolé(e)...

je n'en ai pas.

donnez le prix.

autre choix?
prix?

© BBC Enterprises Ltd 1994

124 **5**

vous avez acheté:
yaourt
viande
pain
salade

vous avez dépensé: 28 F

vous avez acheté:
croissants
tarte (pomme)
clémentines
beurre
fraises

vous avez dépensé: 98 F

vous avez acheté:
cacahuètes
baguette
éclairs (chocolat)
olives

vous avez dépensé: 51 F

vous avez acheté:
fromage
lait
huile
cacahuètes

vous avez dépensé: 45 F

vous avez acheté:
brioches
éclairs (café)
fromage
oranges

vous avez dépensé: 83 F

vous avez acheté:
gâteau (orange)
pommes
légumes
viande

vous avez dépensé: 82 F

vous avez acheté:
eau
légumes
raisins
vin rouge

vous avez dépensé: 68 F

vous avez acheté:
café
pâtisseries
crème
œufs

vous avez dépensé: 68 F

vous avez acheté:
tarte (kiwi)
bananes
apéritif
pain (campagne)

vous avez dépensé: 97 F

vous avez acheté:
choux
poisson
carottes
bananes

vous avez dépensé: 54 F

vous avez acheté:
légumes
yaourt
œufs
pommes

vous avez dépensé: 42 F

vous avez acheté:
gâteau (ananas)
olives
beurre
huile

vous avez dépensé: 79 F

vous avez acheté:
œufs
papier WC
viande
vin blanc

vous avez dépensé: 79 F

vous avez acheté:
tarte (fraise)
tomates
poissons
vin

vous avez dépensé: 98 F

vous avez acheté:
pain (campagne)
salade
viande
fromage

vous avez dépensé: 77 F

vous avez acheté:
yaourt
poisson surgelé
tomates
journal

vous avez dépensé: 49 F

vous avez acheté:
glace (vanille)
baguette
brioches
papier WC

vous avez dépensé: 38 F

vous avez acheté:
tarte (framboise)
pain (complet)
tomates (3 boîtes)
cerises

vous avez dépensé: 89 F

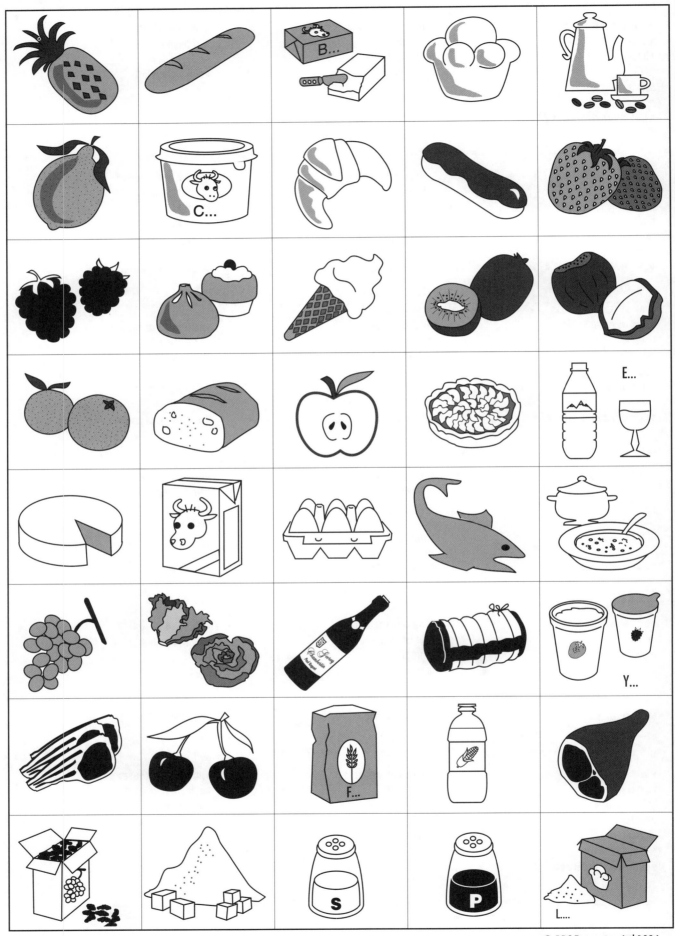

Tomato Rarebit

25g butter
10g flour
20cl milk
tomato purée
little sugar
100g cheese (Cheddar)
1 egg
toast

Pancake batter

125g flour
1 egg
30cl milk
little oil

Apple cake

200g flour
150g caster sugar
75g butter
2 eggs
little milk
little orange
300g apples

Shortbread

100g butter
50g caster sugar
150g flour
little salt

Cheese soufflé

3 eggs
25g butter
30g flour
20cl milk
100g cheese
salt
pepper

Walnut salad

100g nuts
lettuce
oil
vinegar

Bread

40g yeast
30cl water
450g flour
little salt
little olive oil

Welsh Rarebit

grated cheese
little milk
toast

5 127

← turn left	→ turn right	↑ straight ahead
T-junction turn right	T-junction turn left	T-junction ahead/right
T-junction turn left	**STOP**	roundabout
crossroads	P	H
traffic lights	river	5 minutes crossroads
100 m crossroads	500 m crossroads	3 km crossroads

6

vous tournez à gauche	vous tournez à droite	vous allez tout droit
vous prenez la première rue à droite	vous prenez la première rue à gauche	vous prenez la deuxième rue à droite
vous prenez la deuxième rue à gauche	vous arrivez à un stop	jusqu'au rond-point
jusqu'au carrefour	jusqu'au parking	jusqu'à l'hôpital
jusqu'aux feux	vous longez la rivière	c'est à cinq minutes
c'est à cent mètres	c'est à cinq cents mètres	c'est à trois kilomètres

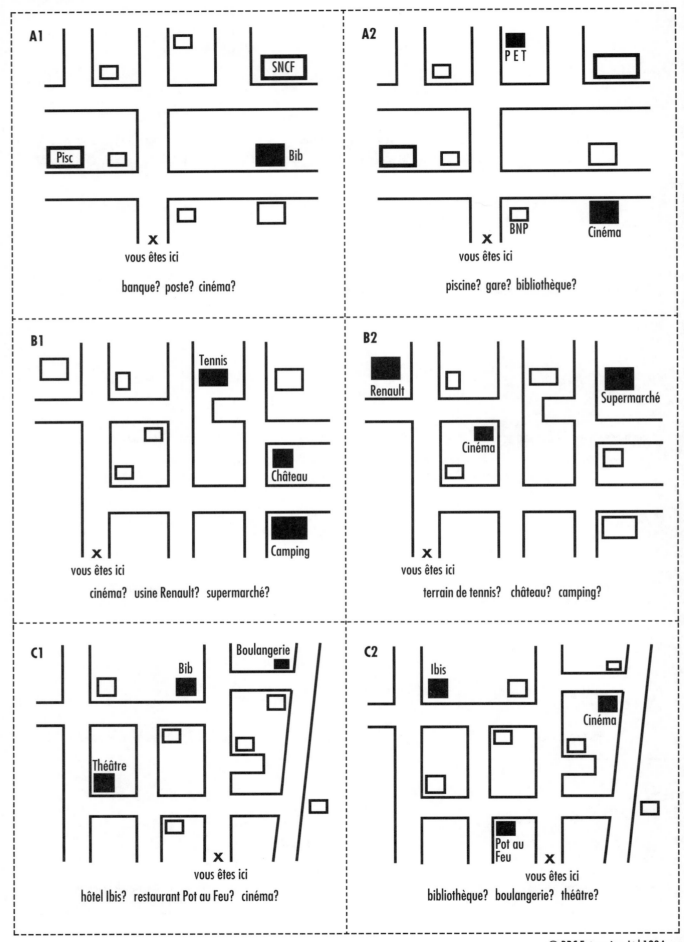

A1

SNCF

Pisc Bib

x
vous êtes ici

banque? poste? cinéma?

A2

PET

BNP Cinéma

x
vous êtes ici

piscine? gare? bibliothèque?

B1

Tennis

Château

Camping

x
vous êtes ici

cinéma? usine Renault? supermarché?

B2

Renault Supermarché

Cinéma

x
vous êtes ici

terrain de tennis? château? camping?

C1

Boulangerie
Bib

Théâtre

x
vous êtes ici

hôtel Ibis? restaurant Pot au Feu? cinéma?

C2

Ibis Cinéma

Pot au
Feu

x
vous êtes ici

bibliothèque? boulangerie? théâtre?

A

Départs quai	2	4	2	4
DIEPPE	8.00	9.06	11.10	13.26
AUFFAY	8.14	—	—	13.40
CLERES	8.40	—	—	14.10
ROUEN	9.16	10.00	12.04	14.50
MANTES-LA-JOLIE	9.41	—	—	—
PARIS ST LAZARE	10.23	10.58	13.02	—

B

Départs		Voie
CHAMBERY	14.35	4
CULOZ	14.55	5
GRENOBLE	15.12	3
LYON PERRACHE	15.23	1
AIX-LES-BAINS	16.49	5

A

Destination	Jour	Heure	A/R?	Pers?	Détails
PARIS	lun	av 12 h	✔	1	vég
LYON	mar	av 14 h	✘	2	—
PARIS	merc	ap 14 h	✔	1	—
LYON	lun	av 12 h	✘	2	1 vég

B

Vols à destination de **Paris**:
    8 h 00 (arrive 9 h 06),
    11 h 20 (arrive 12 h 26),
    15 h 15 (arrive 16 h 31) tous les jours sauf le dimanche.
Prix: 1050 F (adulte) aller-retour;
    600 F aller.

Vols à destination de **Lyon**:
    9 h 12 (arrive 10 h 15),
    12 h 35 (arrive 13 h 45),
    17 h 30 (arrive 18 h 35).
Prix: 950 F (adulte) aller-retour;
    500 F aller.

A1   Vous parlez avec une amie française, Elodie.

départ?   transport?
travail?   temps?

A4   Vous parlez avec une Française, Mme Petit, au restaurant.

départ?   transport?
travail?   temps?

B1   Jouez le rôle d'une amie, Elodie.
travail: secrétaire/bureau

départ: 7 h 45
bus 15″

B4   Jouez le rôle d'une Française, Mme Petit.
Vous êtes au restaurant.
travail: professeur d'espagnol/collège

départ: 7 h 15   métro 25″

A2   Vous parlez avec un ami français, Georges.

départ?   transport?
travail?   temps?

A5   Vous parlez avec une petite Française, Marie-Eve.

départ?   collège
transport?   temps?

B2   Jouez le rôle d'un ami, Georges.
travail: mécanicien/usine

départ: 6 h 30
vélo 35″

B5   Jouez le rôle d'un petit Français, Christophe.
collège

départ: 7 h 45
pied 10″

A3   Vous parlez avec un Français, M. Morlet, au restaurant.

départ?   transport?
travail?   temps?

A6   Vous parlez avec un petit Français, Christophe.

départ?   école
transport?   temps?

B3   Jouez le rôle d'un Français, M. Morlet.
Vous êtes au restaurant.
travail: infirmier/hôpital

départ: 7 h 30
voiture 20″

B6   Jouez le rôle d'une petite Française, Marie-Eve.
école

départ: 8 h 10 – 15
voiture 7/8″

Hôtel	Camping		
170 F			
190 F			
200 F			10 F, 15 F, 20 F
220 F			
250 F			
280 F			
300 F	40 F	55 F	
340 F	45 F	55 F	
360 F	50 F	60 F	0 F, 5 F, 10 F

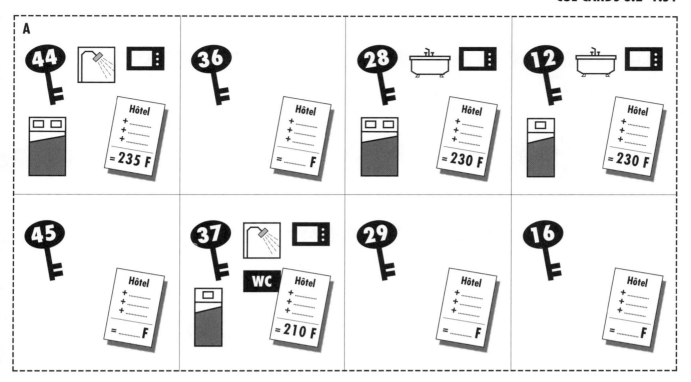

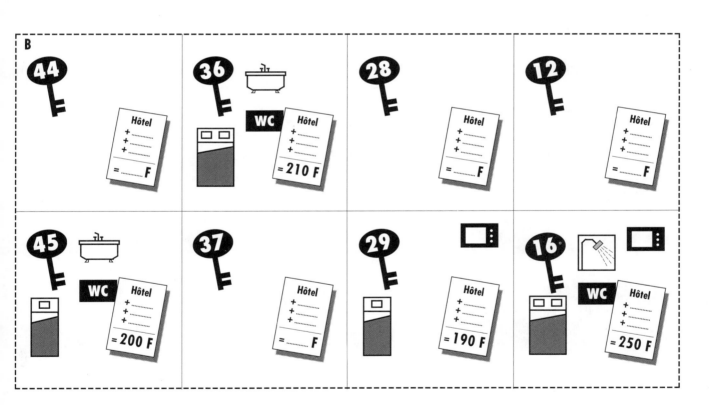

CHOICE FRAMEWORK 8.3   P.52

Raison	Retard	Arrivée
	½ h	8 h 00
	1 h	10 h 00
	1 h ½	12 h 00
	2 h	13 h 00
	45 mn	13 h 30
	3 h	15 h 00
	6 h	20 h 00
	50 mn	23 h 00
		repas? dîner?

PHOTOCOPY MASTER 8.4   P.53

...ne marche pas	Il n'y a pas...	Je pourrais avoir...? Est-ce que je peux avoir...?
	C...	

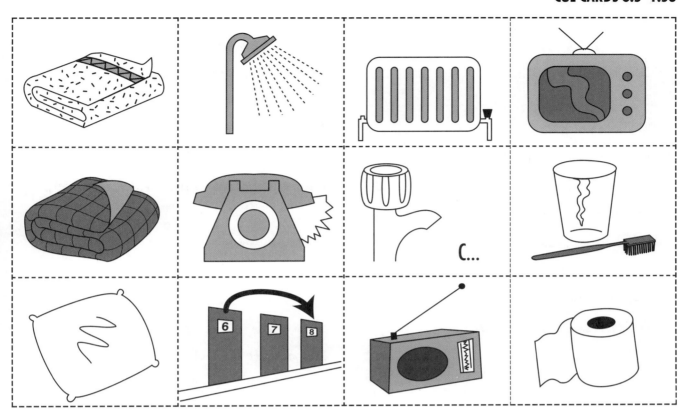

Culturoscope
Using a dictionary for this worksheet tick the appropriate boxes.

	0	*	**	***	****
1 Vous avez un téléphone dans votre chambre.	☐	☐	☐	☐	☐
2 Un tiers des chambres a une salle de bains.	☐	☐	☐	☐	☐
3 Vous avez une chambre de 8m² pour une personne.	☐	☐	☐	☐	☐
4 Vous êtes au troisième étage sans ascenseur.	☐	☐	☐	☐	☐
5 L'hôtel n'a pas de salle de bains privée.	☐	☐	☐	☐	☐
6 Vous n'avez pas de WC privé.	☐	☐	☐	☐	☐
7 Il y a une cabine téléphonique.	☐	☐	☐	☐	☐
8 Vous avez une chambre de 12m² pour deux personnes.	☐	☐	☐	☐	☐
9 Un tiers des chambres n'a pas de salle de bains.	☐	☐	☐	☐	☐
10 Il n'y a pas de téléphone.	☐	☐	☐	☐	☐
11 Vous prenez le petit déjeuner dans votre chambre.	☐	☐	☐	☐	☐
12 La moitié des chambres a un WC.	☐	☐	☐	☐	☐
13 La grande majorité des chambres a une salle de bains et un WC.	☐	☐	☐	☐	☐
14 Vous êtes au troisième étage et vous pouvez monter en ascenseur.	☐	☐	☐	☐	☐

Hôtel-Restaurant Golf de La Carte

1 Name three sports in French. ....

....

2 When is the hotel shut?..

3 Where is the hotel in relation to the local châteaux? ....

....

4 Where is the hotel in relation to Blois? ....

....

5 Quels sont les prix des chambres? ....

6 Quels sont les prix des appartements?................................

7 Le prix du .... est 60 F.

8 L'hôtel est près ....

Château de Beaulieu

1 When is the hotel closed?..

2 How much is breakfast? ....

3 What arrangements apply from November to March? ....

....

Hôtel Groison/Restaurant Jardin du Castel

1 For how long is the hotel closed each year?................................

....

2 Can you have lunch on Sunday in winter? ....

3 L'hôtel a combien de chambres?..

4 Est-ce qu'il se trouve dans le/au centre-ville ou en banlieue?.......

....

5 L'hôtel se trouve dans..

....

Château de l'Aubrière

1 Can you eat at the hotel on Tuesdays? ....

2 Does the hotel close during the year? ....

3 Where is the hotel? ....

4 What is good about swimming there in May? ....

....

5 L'hôtel se trouve dans..

....

CHOICE FRAMEWORK 9.1 P.55

Domicile?	Où?	Avec qui?	Comment?	Nombres d'étages?	Nombres de pièces?	Jardin?	Animaux?
maison	région parisienne	mes parents	grand			oui	mouton(s)
villa	près de Calais	seul(e)	petit			non	lapin(s)
appartement	Rouen	enfants	moderne				poule(s)
château	Presles	partenaire	joli				chien(s)
caravane			calme				chat(s)

				femme
				mari
				mère
				père
				sœur
				frère
				grand(s)-parent(s)
				fils
				fille
				nièce
				neveu
				tante
				oncle
				ami(e)
				seul(e)

A
cinéma?
jeudi?
mercredi?
19 h
devant cinéma

A
venir manger?
samedi?
vendredi?
20.00 h

A
manger au restaurant?
mercredi?
jeudi?
Bistrot Georges?
20.00 h
au restaurant

A
tour à vélo?
samedi?
dimanche?
se retrouver chez moi?
10.00 h

B
cinéma ✔
jeudi ✘
mercredi ✔
heure?
où?

B
manger chez ami ✔
samedi ✘
vendredi ✔
heure?

B
manger au restaurant ✔
mercredi ✘
jeudi ✔
où manger?
heure?
se retrouver?

B
tour à vélo ✔
samedi ✘
dimanche ✔
se retrouver où?
heure?

A

You're a waiter/waitress at a brasserie. Ask the customer the following questions.

— Bonjour, c'est pour manger?

— En salle ou à la terrasse?

— Entendu. Suivez moi. Qu'est-ce que vous allez prendre comme boisson?

— Très bien. Et que désirez-vous manger?

— Je suis désolé(e), mais il n'y a...

— D'accord. Un dessert peut-être?

— Bien. Je reviens tout de suite avec du pain.

B

You've gone into a brasserie for something to eat.

— Respond to the waiter's/waitress's first question.

— Decide where you want to sit.

— Order a drink.

— Order a meal/snack.

— Make a second choice.

— You won't have a dessert.

coq au vin	charcuterie
steak	salade verte
poulet basquaise	salade de tomates ou de carottes
poulet rôti	quiche aux épinards
poulet au citron	quiche aux poivrons
gigot à l'anglaise	quiche aux champignons
escalope de veau à la crème	quiche au jambon
escalope de dinde	quiche aux fruits de mer
cuisse de canard rôtie	pamplemousse rafraîchi
filet de merlu	jambon crû du pays
escalope de saumon	raviolis à la niçoise

Menu à 150 F

1er Plat

La tarte au fromage blanc et aux poireaux

Les 6 huîtres Pleine Mer (suppl. 6 F)

La cassolette de moules marinières

L'assiette du jardinier

La salade de foies de volaille au vinaigre de Xérès

L'éventail de lieu aux condiments

Les six escargots en poêlon (suppl.6 F)

2ème Plat

Le filet de porc rôti à la compote d'oignons

La langue braisée au vinaigre de cidre

Le poulet sauté à la normande

Le filet de colin à la fondue de tomate fraîche

La bavette grillée au beurre de moutarde ancienne

Le faux filet grillé (suppl. + 10 F) ou au poivre (+ 15 F)

L'andouillette de Troyes à la dijonnaise

3ème Plat

Salade, Camembert ou fromage blanc

4ème Plat

Glaces et sorbets variés

Savarin aux fruits frais

Salade de fruits

Tarte aux pommes et aux fruits de saison

Mousse au chocolat

Ile flottante

Tous nos desserts sont préparés Maison

Ce menu est servi tous les jours jusqu'à 21 h 45

Non servi veilles de fêtes, fêtes, samedi soir et dimanche midi

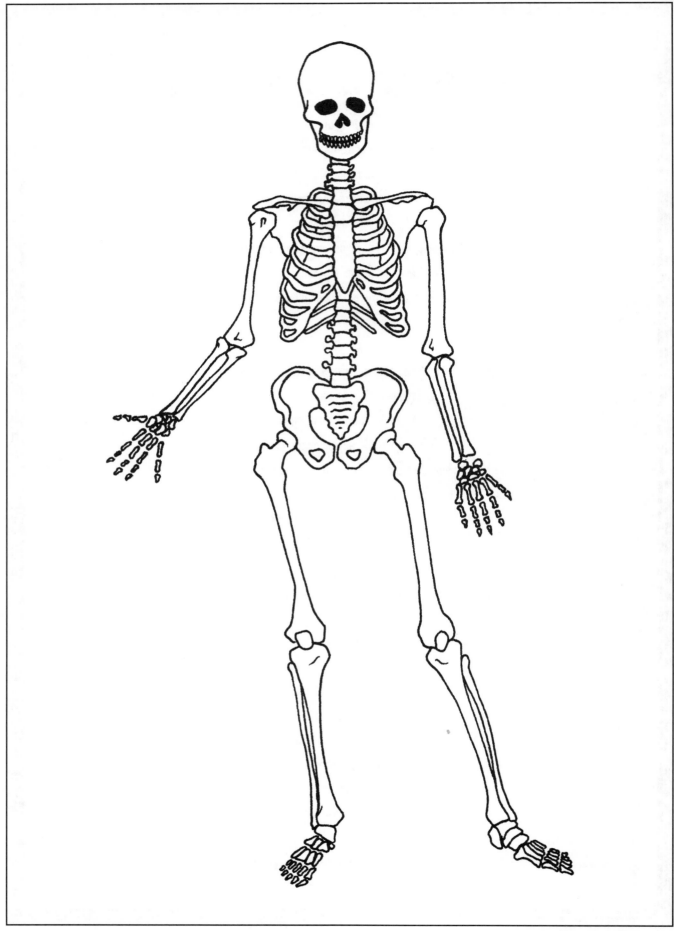

Problème/symptomes		Durée	Gravité	Conseil/Prescription
		2 h	!	
		2 j	!!	
		3 j	!!!	
		4 j		pastilles
				> dentiste
				> docteur
				> H

1A Vous avez un problème.
A vous de choisir:

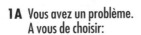

2A Vous avez un problème.
A vous de choisir:

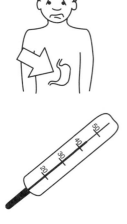

3A Vous avez un problème.
A vous de choisir:

4A Vous avez un problème.
A vous de choisir:

2A Vous êtes pharmacien(ne).
Demandez au client/
à la cliente:
– ses symptômes
– depuis quand?
– la gravité
Recommandez un remède
approprié.

2A Vous êtes pharmacien(ne).
Demandez au client/
à la cliente:
– ses symptômes
– depuis quand?
– la gravité
Recommandez un remède
approprié.

2A Vous êtes pharmacien(ne).
Demandez au client/
à la cliente:
– ses symptômes
– depuis quand?
– la gravité
Recommandez un remède
approprié.

2A Vous êtes pharmacien(ne).
Demandez au client/
à la cliente:
– ses symptômes
– depuis quand?
– la gravité
Recommandez un remède
approprié.

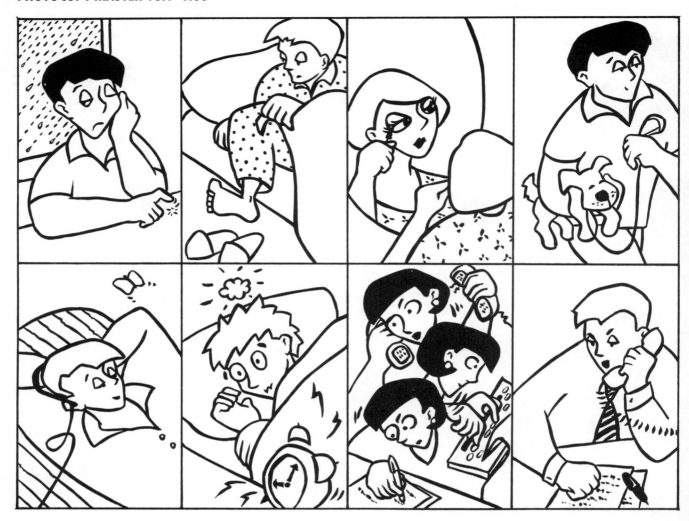

CUE CARDS 13.2 P.83

1A Interviewez B pour savoir: — son nom — où il/elle habite — sa formation (durée, objectifs) — son ambition	**2A** Interviewez B pour savoir: — son nom — où il/elle habite — sa formation (durée, objectifs) — son ambition	**3A** Interviewez B pour savoir: — son nom — où il/elle habite — sa formation (durée, objectifs) — son ambition	**4A** Interviewez B pour savoir: — son nom — où il/elle habite — sa formation (durée, objectifs) — son ambition
1B Répondez aux questions. Voici vos détails: — Emile/Emilie Durand — Paris — BTS tourisme — durée: 2 ans — objectif: travailler en Italie	**2B** Répondez aux questions. Voici vos détails: — Jean/Jeanne Dupont — Toulon — BTS tourisme — durée: 2 ans — objectif: travailler aux Etats-Unis	**3B** Répondez aux questions. Voici vos détails: — Michel/Michelle Plon — Rouen — licence langues étrangères appliquées (ang/esp) — durée: 3 ans — objectif: travailler chez.../ pour... compagnie internationale (Paris?)	**4B** Répondez aux questions. Voici vos détails: — Claude Falcoz — Paris — licence d'anglais — durée: 3 ans — objectif: travailler dans un collège (dans le Midi?)

A1   M./Mme Fournet   Vous téléphonez à M./Mme Leblanc pour fixer un rendez-vous.
lundi	9 h – 12 h réunion
	12 h – 13 h 30 déjeuner
	Madame Bernet
	13 h 30 départ Strasbourg
mardi	Strasbourg toute la journée
mercredi	9 h – 10 h bureau
	10 h – 12 h réunion
	12 h – 14 h déjeuner
	M. Jones
	14 h – 18 h bureau

B1   M./Mme Leblanc   Vous recevez un coup de téléphone de la part de M./Mme Fournet, qui voudrait vous voir cette semaine.
lundi	9 h – 12 h bureau
	12 h – 13 h 30 déjeuner
	14 h – 16 h réunion
mardi	9 h – 12 h bureau
	12 h – 13 h 30 déjeuner avec Marie Durand
mercredi	9 h – 11 h bureau
	11 h départ Paris
	13 h arrive Paris

A2   M./Mme Bousquet   Vous téléphonez à M./Mme Edouard pour fixer un rendez-vous.
lundi	9 h – 11 h réunion
	12 h – 13 h 30 déjeuner
	14 h hôpital
mardi	9 h – 10 h réunion
	10 h – 11 h bureau
	11 h – 12 h dentiste
	12 h 30 déjeuner patron
	14 h – 15 h 30 bureau
	15 h 30 départ Paris
mercredi	Paris

B2   M./Mme Edouard   Vous recevez un coup de téléphone de la part de M./Mme Bousquet, qui voudrait vous voir cette semaine.
lundi	9 h – 12 h bureau
	12 h – 13 h 30 libre
	13 h 30 bureau
mardi	9 h – 10 h bureau
	10 h – 11 h banque
	11 h – 12 h bureau
	12 h – 13 h 30 libre
	13 h 30 – 14 h 30 bureau
	14 h 30 départ Marseille
mercredi	Marseille

A3   M./Mme Pinoteau   Vous téléphonez à M./Mme Bernard pour fixer un rendez-vous.
lundi	Presles toute la journée
mardi	9 h – 12 h bureau
	12 h – 13 h 30 déjeuner
	M. Smith
	13 h 30 – 15 h 30 réunion
	15 h 30 – 17 h 30 bureau
mercredi	9 h – 12 h bureau
	12 h – 13 h 30 libre
	13 h 30 – 15 h réunion
	15 h départ Londres

B3   M./Mme Bernard   Vous recevez un coup de téléphone de la part de M./Mme Pinoteau, qui voudrait vous voir cette semaine.
lundi	9 h – 12 h bureau
	12 h – 13 h 30 déjeuner
	13 h 30 – 17 h bureau
mardi	9 h départ Paris
mercredi	9 h – 10 h bureau
	10 h – 12 h réunion
	12 h – 14 h libre
	14 h départ Marseille

A4   M./Mme Laubier   Vous téléphonez à M./Mme Brun pour fixer un rendez-vous.
lundi	9 h – 12 h bureau
	12 h – 13 h 30 libre
	13 h 30 – 16 h réunion
	16 h – 17 h 30 bureau
mardi	9 h – 12 h visite à Meaux
	12 h – 13 h 30 déjeuner Meaux
	14 h – 17 h 30 bureau
mercredi	Paris toute la journée

B4   M./Mme Brun   Vous recevez un coup de téléphone de la part de M./Mme Laubier, qui voudrait vous voir cette semaine.
lundi	9 h – 12 h réunion
	12 h – 14 h déjeune
	M. Leclerc
	14 h – 17 h 30 bureau
mardi	9 h – 11 h bureau
	11 h banque
	12 h – 13 h 30 déjeuner
	Mme Smith
	13 h 30 – 17 h 30 bureau
mercredi	Meaux toute la journée

Vous me faites un paquet-cadeau?

Virginie Ducreux veut acheter un cadeau. Choisissez la bonne réponse.

1 Virginie est invitée à:
a) déjeuner ce soir ☐
b) dîner ce soir ☐
c) dîner samedi soir ☐

3 Virginie veut dépenser/y mettre:
a) à peu près 100 francs ☐
b) plus de 100 francs ☐
c) pas plus de 100 francs ☐

5 Virginie décide de prendre:
a) des bonbons d'Auvergne ☐
b) un kilo de chocolats ☐
c) une boîte de chocolats maison ☐

2 Les bonbons d'Auvergne coûtent:
a) 86 francs la boîte ☐
b) 76 francs la boîte ☐
c) 96 francs la boîte ☐

4 Les chocolats maison sont faits:
a) dans une maison ☐
b) par la pâtisserie elle-même ☐
c) en Auvergne ☐

A1
Vous voulez acheter un pull.
Couleurs préférées: bleu ou gris
Taille: 40
Prix maximum: 300 francs
Vouz en avez vu en vitrine.

A2
Vous voulez acheter une chemise.
Couleurs préférées: bleu ou vert
Taille: 40 cm (col)
Prix maximum: 250 francs
Vouz en avez vu en vitrine.

A3
Vous voulez acheter des chaussures.
Vous avez trouvé 3 paires que vous aimez.
2 paires sont bleues. 1 paire est marron.
Prix maximum: 500 francs.

A4
Vous voulez acheter une cravate.
Couleurs préférées: bleu, rouge, vert (rayé?)
En soie ou en polyester
Prix maximum: 250 francs
Vouz en avez vu en vitrine.

B1
Vous travaillez dans un magasin.
Un(e) client(e) s'intéresse aux pulls. Vous en avez en rouge,
jaune et bleu marine.
Tailles: de 36 à 44
Prix: normalement 320 francs,
mais cette semaine en solde – 280 francs.

B2
Vous travaillez dans un magasin.
Un(e) client(e) s'intéresse aux chemises.
Vous en avez en vert clair, blanc.
Tailles: 38, 40, 42 cm (col)
Prix: 200 francs, 300 francs.

B3
Vous travaillez dans un magasin de chaussures.
Un(e) client(e) à trouvé 3 paires possibles.
Elles sont toutes en cuir.
Prix: les bleues – 499 francs ou 699 francs;
les marron – 790 francs.

B4
Vous travaillez dans un magasin.
Un(e) client(e) s'intéresse aux cravates.
Vous en avez en vert, bleu, rose.
Prix: soie – 300 francs;
polyester – 200 francs, 150 francs.

1A

Vous avez passé une soirée très agréable chez des amis. Cela s'est très bien passé. Vous téléphonez à votre hôte/hôtesse pour le/la remercier. Vous avez surtout aimé le canard qu'ils ont servi! Leur bébé était un peu souffrant.
Téléphonez pour remercier.

1B

Vous avez reçu dix amis hier soir. Cela s'est très bien passé. Tous les invités vous ont présenté de belles fleurs. Votre bébé a été un peu souffrant, mais il va mieux ce matin.
Le téléphone sonne.

2A

Hier, c'était votre anniversaire. Votre meilleur(e) ami(e) français(e) vous a envoyé un beau paquet. Le cadeau était exactement ce qu'il vous fallait! Téléphonez pour remercier. Vous n'avez pas eu de nouvelles de sa famille depuis Noël.
Téléphonez pour remercier.

2B

Vous êtes français(e). Il y a quinze jours, vous avez envoyé un cadeau à votre meilleur(e) ami(e) anglais(e) pour son anniversaire.
Le téléphone sonne.

3A

Vous avez reçu un beau paquet-cadeau d'un(e) ami(e) français(e). C'est un tableau: un paysage de la région où il/elle habite. Vous appréciez beaucoup. Vous n'avez pas eu de ses nouvelles depuis six mois. Vous n'êtes pas sûr(e), mais votre ami(e) va peut-être divorcer.
Téléphonez pour remercier.

3B

Vous êtes français(e). Vous avez envoyé un cadeau à un(e) ami(e) anglais(e). C'est un tableau. Chez vous, ça ne va pas très bien. Votre partenaire est parti(e) – vous allez divorcer!
Le téléphone sonne.

4A

Hélas, vous êtes hospitalisé(e). Vous vous remettez d'une opération, et vous vous sentez déjà beaucoup plus fort(e) qu'avant. Un(e) ami(e) français(e) vous a envoyé un beau bouquet de fleurs et une bouteille d'alcool.
Téléphonez pour remercier.

4B

Vous avez envoyé une bouteille d'alcool de votre région et un bouquet de fleurs à un(e) ami(e) anglais(e) qui est hospitalisé(e). Vous avez l'impression qu'il/elle va vraiment mal.
Le téléphone sonne.

A
Quel est le climat des différentes saisons dans l'Ariège?
Demandez à votre partenaire.

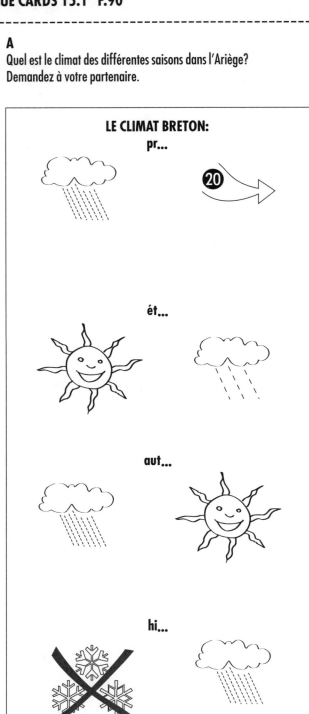

B
Quel est le climat des différentes saisons en Bretagne?
Demandez à votre partenaire.

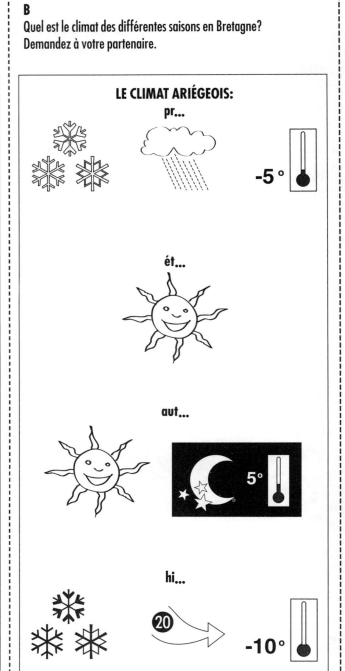

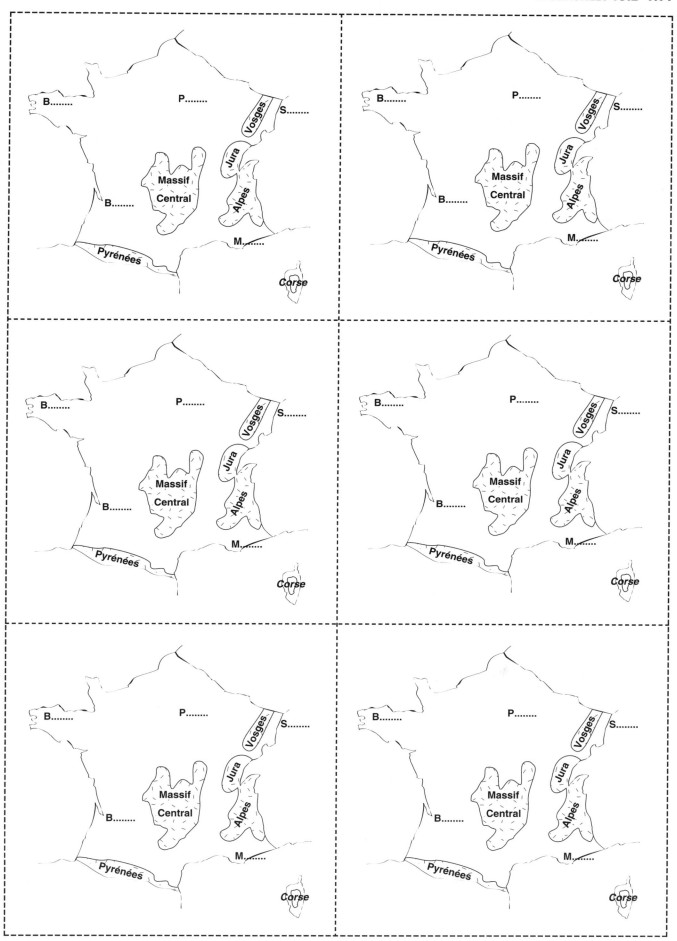

Il y a... ans/Quand j'étais (plus) jeune..../L'année dernière... mais maintenant...

Quoi?	Avec qui? Dans...	Quand?	Où?
	chœur	1 X semaine	chez moi
	club	2 X semaine	dans le voisinage
	ami(e)	l m m j v s d w-e	club
	ami(e)s	saison	terrain de...
	famille	soir	rivière
	femme	matin	lac
	mari	2 X an	pays
	frère	mois	
	sœur		
	fille		
	fils		
	équipe		
	seul(e)		

s'il...

on...

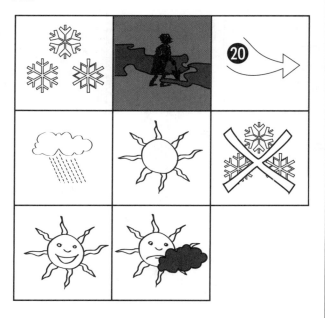

A
Demandez à votre partenaire:
– où il/elle est allé(e) en vacances
– combien de temps il/elle y a passé
– ce qu'on pouvait y faire.

A
Demandez à votre partenaire:
– où il/elle est allé(e) en vacances
– combien de temps il/elle y a passé
– ce qu'on pouvait y faire.

A
Demandez à votre partenaire:
– où il/elle est allé(e) en vacances
– combien de temps il/elle y a passé
– ce qu'on pouvait y faire.

B
Vous avez passé des vacances dans un village des Vosges – quand?
centre de loisirs:

B
Vous avez passé des vacances dans les Alpes – quand?
bonnes pistes; de fond/alpin
centre de loisirs:

B
Vous avez passé des vacances au bord de la mer – quand?

Où	Quand?	Nombre de jours?	Avec qui?	Activités?	Temps?
Italie France Ecosse Pologne Etats-Unis Norvège Belgique Allemagne Autriche Grèce Suisse Alpes Midi Bretagne Paris Edimbourg Florence Prague Le Caire Strasbourg Brighton Turquie	mois saison	X jours dizaine de quinzaine de 3 semaines mois	famille femme mari ami(e) amis frère sœur		

CUE CARDS 16.2 P.95

A Kenya octobre 3 semaines mari/femme animaux fleurs nager	**A** Suisse mars 15 j groupe d'amis ski manger bonne neige	**A** Italie – Florence, Venise avril 10 j **5 jours** ami(e) musées châteaux randonnées manger **5 jours**
B où? quand? nombre de jours? avec? activités? temps?	**B** où? quand? nombre de jours? avec? activités? temps?	**B** où? quand? nombre de jours? avec? activités? temps?

TÉLÉTRAVAIL
Comment gagner sa vie en restant chez soi?

Vous en avez assez de passer trois heures par jour dans les transports pour vous rendre à votre travail? Vous n'arrivez pas à concilier vie de famille et horaires de bureau? Vous voudriez vivre à la campagne? Vous habitez un village et il n'y a pas de travail à des kilomètres à la ronde?

Dans tous ces cas-là, le télétravail est peut-être la solution pour vous. La France compte actuellement 16 000 télétravailleurs et devrait voir grimper ce chiffre entre 300 000 et 500 000 postes d'ici dix ans. Selon la Sofres, 54% des actifs se disent favorables à une activité partielle ou totale à domicile.

Le télétravail, qu'est-ce que c'est?

Vous travaillez chez vous, avec un ordinateur, un fax, un Minitel et une ligne téléphonique professionnelle, c'est l'équipement de base.

Grâce à cette installation, vous restez en contact permanent avec votre employeur. Vous effectuez des travaux de secrétariat, de traduction, de gestion, de comptabilité, d'archivage, de graphisme, etc. La liste est longue!

Suggérez-le à votre employeur.

Il sera peut-être ravi de gagner de la place dans ses bureaux et financera alors l'installation informatique à votre domicile, ainsi que la prise en charge des télécommunications. Un investissement intéressant lorsqu'on songe qu'un poste de télétravailleur peut faire économiser de 48 000 F à 100 000 F par an à une entreprise (économie de surface immobilière, frais de transport, tickets restaurant, etc.).

Martine Kurz

Read the text on page 202 of your book and find the island to match each statement.

1 En été il y a jusqu'à six liaisons ....

2 Il y a une réserve ornithologique ....

3 Monsieur Ramon loue des vélos ....

4 On peut y aller en hélicoptère ....

5 Il y a plusieurs kilomètres de sentiers sur lesquels on peut se promener. ....

6 Il faut apporter des provisions ....

7 La traversée dure dix minutes ....

8 Les départs ont lieu toutes les demi-heures en été ....

9 On peut passer quelques jours en contemplation ....

10 La traversée dure une heure ....

11 Le musée montre un intérieur traditionnel ....

12 Il y a de longues pistes pour faire des tours de vélo ....

13 On part de Lorient ....

14 On part de Granville ....

15 On peut regarder le fond de la mer ....

16 On ne peut pas louer de vélos ....

17 Le voyage dure deux heures quinze minutes ....

18 On part de Quiberon ....

19 Il n'y a pas d'épicerie ....

A1
Téléphonez au camping pour faire une réservation.

une tente
05.07 – 08.07. (3 nuits)
2 personnes

A2
Téléphonez à l'auberge de jeunesse pour faire une réservation.

09.08. – 10.08. (2 nuits)
2 adultes
2 enfants
draps fournis?
petit déjeuner compris?
douches chaudes?

A3
Téléphonez à l'Hôtel Robespierre pour faire une réservation.

01.08. – 06.08. (5 nuits)
2 adultes
1 enfant
petit déjeuner compris?
garage?

A4
Téléphonez à l'auberge de jeunesse pour faire une réservation.

12.07. – 15.07. (3 nuits)
1 adulte
12 enfants
draps fournis
TV?
douches dans les chambres?

B1
Vous travaillez à l'accueil du camping.
Le téléphone sonne.

Il y a des emplacements pour le mois de juillet.

B2
Vous travaillez à l'accueil à l'auberge de jeunesse.
Le téléphone sonne.

Vous êtes complet pour le mois de juillet mais vous avez de la place pour le mois d'août. Les draps sont fournis. Le petit déjeuner n'est pas compris dans le prix (15 francs par personne). Douches chaudes.

B3
Vous travaillez à la réception à l'Hôtel Robespierre.
Le téléphone sonne.

Le petit déjeuner est compris dans le prix des chambres.

L'hôtel se trouve à 100 m d'un parking.

B4
Vous travaillez à la réception de l'auberge de jeunesse.
Le téléphone sonne.

Vous avez de la place pour le mois de juillet. Il y a des douches chaudes à l'étage. Pas de TV. Les draps sont fournis.

A
Votre partenaire est allé(e) au marché. Interviewez-le/-la pour savoir:

quel marché?
quand?
ce qu'il/elle a vu
ce qu'il/elle a acheté.

A
Votre partenaire est allé(e) au marché. Interviewez-le/-la pour savoir:

quel marché?
quand?
ce qu'il/elle a vu
ce qu'il/elle a acheté.

A
Votre partenaire est allé(e) au marché. Interviewez-le/-la pour savoir:

quel marché?
quand?
ce qu'il/elle a vu
ce qu'il/elle a acheté.

A
Votre partenaire est allé(e) au marché. Interviewez-le/-la pour savoir:

quel marché?
quand?
ce qu'il/elle a vu
ce qu'il/elle a acheté.

B1
Vous êtes allé(e) au marché.
– Petticoat Lane
– dimanche matin
– regardé la brocante
– achats: des livres d'occasion, un vieil appareil photo

B2
Vous êtes allé(e) au marché.
– Puces de Montreuil
– dimanche matin
– regardé la brocante
– achats: un masque en bois africain (150 francs)

B3
Vous êtes allé(e) au marché.
– Raspail
– vendredi matin
– regardé fruits et légumes exotiques
– achats: rien

B4
Vous êtes allé(e) au marché.
– Portobello Road
– samedi matin
– regardé la brocante et les antiquités
– achats: dix vieilles cuillers à café

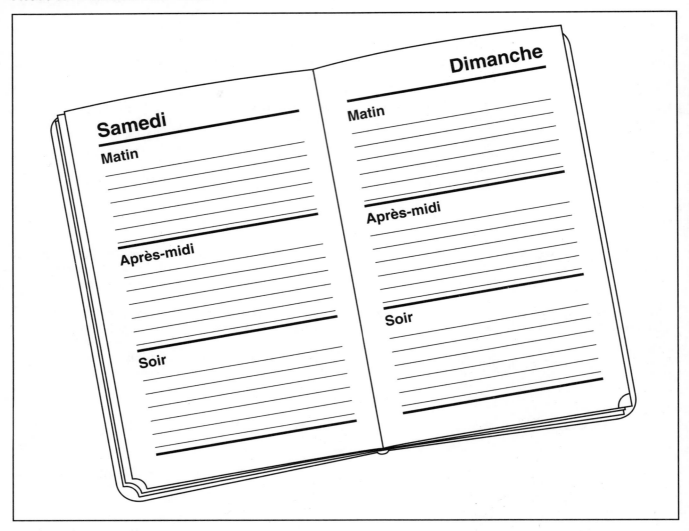

PHOTOCOPY MASTER 20.1 P.107